The Mainieri Factor

Promoting Baseball With a Passion From Miami Dade to Notre Dame, LSU and the Chicago Cubs

By Dr. Demie J. Mainieri

With Additions By Paul D. Mainieri

Forward By Hall of Famer Tommy Lasorda

authorHOUSE

AuthorHouse™
1663 Liberty Drive, Suite 200
Bloomington, IN 47403
www.authorhouse.com
Phone: 1-800-839-8640

© 2007 Demie Mainieri with additions by Paul D. Mainieri. All rights reserved.

No part of this book may be reproduced, stored in a retrieval system, or transmitted by any means without the written permission of the author.

First published by AuthorHouse 12/10/2007

ISBN: 978-1-4343-4235-5 (sc)
ISBN: 978-1-4343-4234-8 (hc)

Printed in the United States of America
Bloomington, Indiana

This book is printed on acid-free paper.

Cover images are courtesy of Steve Franz of the LSU Athletics Department, Photographer Joe Brown, and USA Baseball.

Dedication

To my lovely wife Rosetta, my five children and five grandchildren, my late mother, my late brother Sonny, my former players, and all the other altruistic people who were instrumental in my having a rewarding career and life.

Table of Contents

Foreword   v
Introduction   vii
   Why I Wrote this Book

Chapter 1   1
   The Early Years and How They Affect Your Coaching Career

Chapter 2   9
   Making Your Experiences Work for You, Even When "Uncle Sam Calls"

Chapter 3   17
   Securing a Position – Being in the Right Place at the Right Time: From Coaching In the Army to Miami Dade Community College

Chapter 4   29
   Building a Successful Program: The Miami Dade Community College Story

Chapter 5   51
   Destiny as a Factor in Securing a Position: From Coaching at Columbus High School to the University of Notre Dame

Chapter 6   59
   Building a Power at the University of Notre Dame

Chapter 7   67
   A Potpourri of Stories

Chapter 8   119
   The Relationship between Amateur Baseball and Professional Baseball: The Role of the Scout, the Coach and Parents

Chapter 9   125
   I Did It My Way

The Final Word 129
Epilogue 137
About the Authors 139
   Demie Mainieri
   Paul Mainieri

Foreword

I have known Demie Mainieri since 1968. We met at an American Baseball Coaches Convention. One of his former aspirants Bob Stinson played for me at Ogden, Utah when I was a minor league manager in the Los Angeles Dodgers organization.

It is common knowledge in professional baseball that Demie Mainieri has coached numerous players at Miami Dade Community College who have gone on to play in the major leagues. Some of the most notable have been Bucky Dent, John "Mickey" Rivers, Hall of Famer Steve Carlton, Kurt Bevacqua, Randy Bush, Warren Cromartie, John Cangelosi, Oddibe McDowell, Bob Stinson, and Mike Piazza.

It has always been my feeling that Demie Mainieri displayed the qualities necessary for success in coaching. The recruitment and development of the players under his tutelage are a testament to his coaching prowess. In fact, I was so impressed with his program at Miami Dade that I sent my nephew Eddie Lasorda and Mike Piazza to play for him.

I have been the keynote speaker three times at his Annual Celebrity Golf Tournament at the Doral Country Club and his Kids' Baseball Clinics on the Miami Dade campus.

In addition, I was very instrumental in his son Paul's selection as the head baseball coach at the Air Force Academy and at the University of Notre Dame. I was overjoyed to learn that Paul collaborated with his dad on this book. He has developed the University of Notre Dame into a national power under tremendous odds. Many people in baseball said it could not be done- that a national power couldn't be developed at a northern university. He proved these experts incorrect! He took his 2002 Notre Dame team to the College World Series. The last Notre Dame team to go to the College World Series was forty-five years ago! I am certain that he has made many noteworthy contributions to this book.

The Mainieri family has been very close to me over the years. In fact, I am the Godfather for Paul's youngest son, Thomas.

I am absolutely convinced that you will gain tremendously from reading this book. The authors' vast knowledge and success as college coaches are legendary.
  Tommy Lasorda

Introduction

Why I Wrote this Book

This book should have been written in 1978 while some of my former players from Miami Dade Community College were making a name for themselves in Major League Baseball. Bucky Dent and Mickey Rivers were members of the New York Yankees World Series championship team. Steve Carlton was establishing himself as a future Hall of Famer and four times Cy Young winner. At that time, the book may have had more universal appeal. Nevertheless, the stories I could have told then about those players are still very entertaining and hold just as much, if not more, meaning today.

Back around 1978, people always told me, "Doc, you should write a book, you have so many stories to tell." But the time wasn't right. I didn't want to write a book on baseball skills and practices. I wanted a book that would teach basic principles of coaching philosophy, securing a position, and motivation, based on the success surrounding my thirty years as a college baseball coach and athletic administrator. I wanted to reinforce these principles with real-life stories. I did this while I was an adjunct professor at St. Thomas University and the U.S. Sports Academy, but I waited to write the book.

I think the time to write finally arrived. Mike Piazza, one of my former players, continues to put up Hall of Fame numbers. My oldest son, Paul, has proven that you can develop a winning program at a northern university. His 2002 University of Notre Dame team beat number one ranked Florida State in the N.C.A.A Super Regional in Tallahassee and went on to the College World Series. He has penned part of this book in order to give you some insight into his coaching world. In addition, my other children, Rosemarie, Cathy, John and Jim, collaborated with us, giving us suggestions and reminding me of stories I may have forgotten. My wife, Rosetta, was a tremendous help in reading and revising this manuscript. Tom Crane, an attorney and media executive, who played football with my oldest son Paul at Columbus High School in Miami, FL, gave us some other valuable suggestions. Baseball Historian Cappy Gagnon of Notre Dame also helped and his recommendations were graciously accepted. Pete La Fleur, Assistant Sports Information Director/ Baseball Contact at Notre Dame provided valuable statistics. Jay Rokeach, Sports Information Director at Miami Dade Community College, provided important information for this book. Paul's oldest son, Nicholas, a reserve catcher on the Notre Dame Baseball team and English major, gave us the final impetus for making this book a reality. His technical writing and typing skills were welcomed and appreciated. Bill Franques of LSU and Jon Lineback of Author House were very helpful down the stretch. What I am saying, in other words, is that I don't think I could have written this book in 1978, because I would not have had the help and support of all these people. By waiting until 2005 and finishing it in 2007, I was finally able to put together the right book, with their assistance, and I only hope the reader finds it both entertaining and educational.

                Demie John Mainieri

Photo: Courtesy of Bob Bailey of Miami Dade

Chapter 1

The Early Years and How They Affect Your Coaching Career

The early years of your life have a profound influence on you as it relates to your philosophies and what type of coach you might become later on. I firmly believe this after considering the early portion of my life.

My parents both migrated from Italy in the latter part of the 19th century. My father was 19 years old when he came to the United States. He came with only 18 cents in his pocket and his parents remained in Italy. My mother was six years old when she came over with her parents, a sister and a brother. Ultimately, they married and settled in Jersey City, New Jersey, which is located across the Hudson River from New York City.

I was the youngest of 11 children, but that was ok because believe it or not, my father made a pretty good living as a blacksmith. In fact, at the height of his earning power, he owned his blacksmith shop, a tavern, an Italian restaurant and delicatessen and an apartment complex. He made his money by servicing the horses used by the police department, garbage collectors, and the men delivering ice.

When my father was only 45, he came down with a sever case of Parkinson's disease and was rendered unable to work. His entire right side, including his leg, hand, and lip shook uncontrollably. At this point in his life, I had not been born yet so I found out later when the condition came about. My mother told me it started soon after he was beaten up with a lead pipe and thrown in an alley by some thugs because he would not agree to pay the "protection" money and unionize his blacksmith shop.

With the great Depression coming soon after this unfortunate incident, my father lost all of his businesses. My eight sisters and two brothers had to work in order to keep our home. My mother was too proud to go on relief to get help. My sisters, the oldest of which was 24 years older than me, paved the way for the younger children.

As I grew up and attended school, my teachers were constantly telling me that I talked too much in class. My reputation as a talker followed me throughout my elementary school years until eighth grade, when I had a teacher named Mrs. Grimsley. She told me she would judge me on what I did in her class and not on what she heard from other teachers. What a great woman! This very intelligent teacher taught me a lot by taking this approach, something that I never forgot through my years of coaching and teaching youngsters.

Due to my father's disability and age when I was born, I didn't grow up with a normal father-son relationship. I never got to play catch or do anything else with him. This void in my life was filled by Sonny, my older brother. When I was 9 he enrolled me in the Young Men's Christian Association, a place that helped me a lot since I came from a pretty rough neighborhood.

We lived in a predominately Irish Catholic area and as a kid you would be commonly called a "dirty wop," "dago," "spaghetti bender," "grease ball" and so forth. I would go home to tell my mother that the neighborhood kids were calling me such names. She would say, "Demie, sticks and stones will break your bones but names will never hurt you." She told me this so many times that it was a good many years before I found out she hadn't coined the phrase. Only after I married did my wife Rosetta tell me that comment was a long standing phrase.

As I got older though, you had to be able to use your hands to survive that environment. We didn't have any gangs like you see all over the place now, just groups of tough talking individuals. We had competition between the neighborhoods in stickball. We use to play for twenty-five cents to one dollar a man. You can imagine these games got pretty heated. What a way to learn how to handle pressure!

My YMCA experience was pivotal in my early childhood because I was around people who came from some very stable home situations. The YMCA back in those days was predominately a Protestant organization, so it was a very gratifying experience to be treated well and enjoy my time there as an Italian-American Catholic kid. While at the Y, I participated in every sport offered. I was on the boxing team, the gymnastics team, and the swimming team as a diver. I also played all the team sports. The Y, at that time, was tied into Springfield College (MA) and I remember a team of physical educators and health professionals coming from that college periodically to give us a battery of physical fitness tests. I tested as the highest in my group frequently and more importantly these professionals encouraged me, to seriously consider becoming a coach and physical educator some day. This was the push I needed.

My days at the Y had a profound impact on my character development. Many kids back in the neighborhood where I lived may have had better athletic ability than I had but they were never put in the proper setting to develop.

In elementary school on Friday afternoons they would show movies in the auditorium. Each student had to pay ten cents in order to attend and if you didn't have the money, you stayed in the classroom. Steve Berezney, one of my good friends, and I used to give five cents each to a kid in our class so he could attend the movie. The importance of altruism was something I learned early from my parents.

When the ice cream truck came into our neighborhood, my father would never allow my eight sisters to eat ice cream in front of the other neighborhood children, who may not have had the money to buy any. He would give my oldest sister enough money to buy all the children on the block ice cream. Examples like these are what I grew up around, so never forget how your actions can make an impression on your kids and other youngsters around you.

After graduating from elementary school, Steve Berezney and I enrolled in Dickinson High School, which was the biggest high school in Jersey City. My other friends, Frank and Jim Vitale, enrolled in Lincoln High School, a much smaller school, which had only college preparatory and general education curricula.

At the time of our initial enrollment at Dickinson, Steve Berezney's oldest brother was playing for the Green Bay Packers. He had been a former great at Dickinson and later at Fordham University, then a powerhouse in the college ranks. In fact, as youngsters, we had the opportunity to view on the sidelines the championship game between the Packers and the Giants.

At Dickinson, Steve and I both went out for the football team. I thought that I was doing pretty well for a skinny little freshman kid. I played quarterback and had a pretty good arm, but after a week or so of pre-season drills, the student manager came up to me and said he needed my uniform back because they didn't have enough to go around. There was a new player on the team, Sam Lupo, who needed my uniform. He was a big strong lineman. I was devastated.

The head coach was a dentist by the name of Dr. Peters. I was crushed simply because I felt that the head coach should have at least given me a better chance to make the club or at least talked to me personally before releasing me from the team. My friend Steve made the team, and I was happy for him but never the less was still hurt and confused.

As a result of this experience, I vowed that if I ever became a coach, I would never cut or release a player without talking to the released individual personally.

Years later, I was able to put the situation in perspective when Sam Lupo went on to play at William and Mary, and Dr. Peters was spending more time in the dental office because he had been fired after one year as Head Football Coach.

On the way home from that last football workout, I met my brother, Sonny, who was home on furlough from the Army Air Corp. He was an officer because he graduated from the Aviation Cadet School at the beginning of World War II. I met my brother on Journal Square and he asked why I was not at football. I told him the bad news and I will never forget what he said to me.

He said, "Demie, that's alright. We will transfer you to Lincoln High School and show the people at Dickinson what a mistake they made."

Sonny was my hero for many reasons. He flew twenty-five missions over Germany during World War II. Later, while still in the Air Force he received his Batchelor of Science degree, and after that completed his Masters in Business Administration. He retired from the Air Force as a Colonel. So what he said to me that day on Journal Square really lifted me, hit home, and inspired me that I really could do well.

I had to use my sister Carmela's address, which was in the Lincoln High School district, in order to transfer. During my first year at Lincoln my sister Julie died at the age of thirty-five from cancer. Julie always stressed to me the importance of getting an education.

Lincoln High School was just coming off a state championship season under Coach Bill Cochrane. The team's great running back was Lloyd Skinner, also a state tumbling champion.

Coach Cochrane had drills in the gymnasium. He also knew that I was a promising tumbler on the gymnastics team, since my brother Sonny had encouraged me into the sport, in order to build my strength and flexibility. Coach Cochrane felt he might have another super star on his hands like Lloyd Skinner. Even though I never reached super star status, coach did work me as a backup that year to the regular quarterback, Willie Garguilo.

During the spring of my freshman year coach Cochrane, also the head baseball coach played me as the regular shortstop. During this period many military veterans had returned home to finish high school. I can remember a stylish left hand pitcher by the name of Marshall Jacobs, who looked great throwing in the gymnasium. Since Marshall looked so good, Coach Cochrane started him in our first game outside against Union Hill High School. In the first inning, Union Hill was hitting rockets all over the field. First pitch was a three base hit, the second pitch was a home run, and the third pitch a double. Coach Cochrane called time for a conference on the mound with the pitcher, Garguilo the catcher, and me. Prior to getting to the mound, Coach Cochrane asked Garguilo "What does this guy have?"

Garguilo responded, "I don't know coach. I haven't caught one of his pitches yet!"

I learned valuable lesson about the difference between practice and game players!

My sophomore year in football, I didn't see much action on another great Lincoln High School team that played St. Cecilia High School, coached by Vince Lombardi, in the Liberty Bowl.

The next year Bill Cochrane became head football and baseball coach at St. Peters Preparatory School, which was and continues to be, a very prestigious Jesuit high school in New Jersey. I was elated when he asked me to transfer to St. Peters. But as a junior, I would have had to make-up two years of Latin, so it didn't appear feasible to transfer. Finishing my career at Lincoln turned out to be a wise move because I ended up with a fairly successful athletic career. I had some of my best games against Dickinson High School in both football and baseball. In addition, I played in two post-season All-Star football games. Bill Cochrane coached the first one in 1945 and in 1946 the coach was Tony Siano, a former Fordham University great.

At Lincoln High School, my athletic locker was between Rufus "Roy" Hamilton, who was a track star that became a very popular singer, and Andy Stanfield who became an Olympic sprint champion. Both of them were African-Americans and we had many conversations on how to develop harmony between races. This was a great experience in race relations that would help me during my entire career and life.

I told you all of this to show how I came to be the coach and person I became. If it were not for Sonny's encouragement and Coach Cochrane's giving me a chance, I may have never had the opportunity to be an athlete. Bill Cochran, and his approach to coaching, was a positive influence on my future career, as he was a great organizer and motivator. He certainly gave me the motivation to pursue a college education. Without my experiences in athletics, I probably would have never gotten a college education, a master's degree and eventually a doctoral degree from Columbia University. In my lifetime, numerous people have, and will continue to have, an integral hand in my career and life. There is no doubt in my mind that I have been blessed.

Summary of Possible Development of Philosophical and Psychological Principles to Be Used In Coaching

(1) Judge athletes not on their physical attributes but by the size of their heart as indicated by their work ethic and desire to excel. It is so easy to follow the philosophy that "big athletes" have to prove they can't play and "small athletes" have to prove that they can play. It is a continuing challenge but face it with conviction!

(2) Establish a sound defensible principle to follow when dismissing players from the team. Make objective decisions with the best interests of the team in mind not based on an emotional attachment to a particular player or players. The easiest way to release a player or players is to post a "cut or release list" or a list of players who have made the team. The more professional way would be to talk to each individual involved. This approach is very time consuming but players that come out for your team deserves this courtesy. There may be times that you may want to consider keeping a prospective player out for the team indefinitely and allow the player to eliminate himself. On a few occasions, some players may just over come all odds and make your team which would be a great boost to that person's self esteem. You can't make decisions based on what is politically correct but at least have some dialogue with the player. Many times the limits placed on team travel size and limited lockers available negate the aforementioned happening.

(3) Judge people based not on what other people say about them but how they act and perform for you. Don't be afraid to give a person a second chance. As coaches we are first and foremost teachers and are in the business of trying to help youngsters, under our tutelage, to achieve success in life.

(4) Judge people, not on the color of their skin, their ethnicity, or religion but by their ability and character.

(5) Try to judge person's make up- the intangibles. Later in this book, you will see more specific examples of the importance of these traits and ways in which they can be recognized and evaluated.

Chapter 2

Making Your Experiences Work for You, Even When "Uncle Sam Calls"

1947. AFTER GRADUATING FROM LINCOLN High School I didn't have all of the core subjects to enter a senior college. In view of this problem, I had to take a course in geometry and physics at night school that fall. After successfully completing these courses, I matriculated and completed one semester at Seton Hall University which was close to my home in Jersey City.

That spring I received a letter from Dr. Dudley DeGroot, Head Football Coach at West Virginia University. He inquired as to whether or not I was still interested in playing football at West Virginia University. I was. But as a transfer student, I would have to sit out one year of activity. So rather than go that route, he arranged a football grant-in-aid for me to Potomac State College of West Virginia University.

While at Potomac State I played football and baseball. During the football season, I had a head and neck injury that ended my football career. But after finishing my athletic career at Potomac State, I transferred to West Virginia University, where I received a Bachelor of Science Degree in Health and Physical Education.

Me, while quarterback at Potomac State College.

I graduated from college in 1952, during the height of the Korean War, so I decided it would be best to complete my military obligation immediately. I was very fortunate to have finished my college education because I had a draft deferment. This was particularly significant to me since two people very close to me, teammates from the football team at Lincoln High School, Tom Mc Gill and Ted Koslowski, were killed in action.

I ended up volunteering for the Army and took my medical basic at Camp Pickett, Virginia. With my degree in health and physical education, I was selected to teach the future medics about the various drugs used in the field when treating the wounded. Since I didn't have a background in this area, I had to do a lot of reading and preparation in order to not embarrass myself.

After completing basic training, I was one of eight soldiers out of over seven hundred troops that were sent to the European Theatre. The remaining enlisted men were all sent to the Far East. Years later, while working on my doctoral degree at Columbia University, I met a fellow who took basic training with me at Camp Pickett and was sent to Korea. He told me that seventy-five percent of the group from Camp Pickett that was sent to Korea was killed in *the first day of combat*. To this day, I don't doubt that my being sent to Europe was the result of divine intervention.

After landing in Germany, I had the choice of being assigned to a hospital in Germany or a hospital in France as a rehabilitation specialist. I went to France, partially because when you think of France, you naturally think of Paris. Once there, however, I found out how misguided my thoughts were.

Some events, however bleak, can turn out for the best. This is something I learned while in France, and it is something you should also learn and never forget. Looking at things in a positive manner and having a strong faith helps you to cope with the vicissitudes of life.

My dreams of Paris were immediately dashed when I was assigned to the Twenty-Eight General Hospital in La Rochelle, France. The housing area for single enlisted men was located in Croix Chapeau, a tent city located outside La Rochelle, rural living in every sense of the word.

After being processed by the personnel department, I found out the Army hospital did not have a rehabilitation department. I was put on temporary duty working a rock pile. I assure you, the job wasn't as thrilling as it sounds. It consisted of moving rocks from one pile to another and another, just to keep you busy. The sergeant in charge informed the workers that, if they weren't happy, they could volunteer to serve in Korea. That was how I kept things in perspective. All in all, I was pretty lucky.

I was eventually assigned to the Special Services Department under a Lieutenant Clifford Ross. After working there a couple of weeks, I was notified that his department was over staffed and I would be re-assigned. I had read in the Stars and Stripes that the Army would be starting a regimental level baseball program in this area of France. Since Ross was going to be the Head Baseball Coach of the team, I asked him if it would be possible for me to remain in his Special Services Department until he had try-outs for the baseball team. He approved my request. After a two week try-out, I made the team and was placed on temporary duty (TDY) to play baseball on the La Rochelle Comets. This opportunity would not only drastically change my life in the Army but my future outside the Army.

My experience on the baseball team was a great experience. I played second base because our shortstop was a player from Baltimore, Maryland. He was a bonus baby who had signed with the Boston Red Sox before he was drafted into the Army. Since I had always played on the left side of the infield, I learned how to turn a double play as a second basemen.

As the baseball season was coming to an end, I read in the Stars and Stripes that the command where I was stationed was also starting a regimental football program. The article also stated that Dr. Dudley DeGroot, former West Virginia University and University of New Mexico head football coach was coming to Croix Chapeau, France as a Department of the Army civilian, to put on a football coaching clinic. I couldn't believe it.

I met Dr. DeGroot after he arrived and he asked me what I was doing over there. I told him I was in the Army.

After I told him this, he turned to General Gallagher and said, "I'll do your clinic, but here is your coach. I recruited this young man when I coached at West Virginia."

General Gallagher told me, "Come to my office on Monday with a plan to win a championship."

What an amazing break!

On the baseball team, I played with a catcher named John Delli Santi, who had played baseball and football at Fordham University. During John's tenure at Fordham, the football program was well respected and was considered to be one of the better football programs in the country. I asked John if he would help me with the new football team, because he also had some head coaching experience at a high school in New Jersey. He was an ideal person to work with. But we got right down to work, only having a weekend to come up with a plan!

We decided early on that we were going to go first class and do everything possible to satisfy the General. We were concerned that if our plan was too grandiose, General Gallagher might throw us out of his office. But we decided to go for it, realizing that going back to the "rock detail" was a strong possibility.

    Some of the salient points as I can recall were:
(1) we would have one head coach and three assistants
(2) we needed a trainer, equipment manager, and media person
(3) we would need a staff car to visit all the Army bases in our command
(4) we would need permission to check personnel files(201 files) of all the troops
(5) we wanted to bring up to one hundred prospects on temporary duty(TDY) to Croix Chapeau for up to two weeks for try-outs
(6) we would select fifty-five players and place them on temporary duty until the end of the season
(7) all coaches and support personnel were to be on temporary duty and placed under the supervision of the post commander

    We presented this to General Gallagher and his staff. It was approved with a reminder that we better win. Right from the get go we were under incredible pressure. The thought of the rock detail was great motivation not to fail.

    John Delli Santi and I were a great fit. John coached the line and I had the backfield and another guy named Mel Warren coached the ends. Gil Thomas, my buddy from the baseball team, was the equipment manager and Bob Bolin was the trainer. We were able to get a person with experience in the print media as our sports information director.

    We recruited some pretty good football players. Some of them came from major football colleges and some came from small colleges. A few of them came with only high school experience. We even had our version of Buddy Young and Glen Davis. Both were outstanding backs that shared the last names, even though they were not related to the famous Buddy and Glen.

    We opened our season at the Bordeaux Municipal Stadium (where the Olympics were held) in front of some 25,000 people! What a great experience. We won the game against another Army team 35-0.

We went on to a 9-0 regular season as we won the Championship of Southern France. We lost to a great Army team from Northern France in the All France Championship game.

After this, I never went back to rock pile detail. I remained in Special Services for the duration of my time in the Army. I met some great people like Colonel Lentz, former West Pointer and classmate of President Eisenhower, who was in charge of the special services for the entire command. He was my mentor and was like a father to me during a very difficult period in my life. Lt. Ron Mutti, the officer who traveled with our teams, was a great friend and advisor. All in all I was extremely blessed and very lucky.

After the end of the football season, I flew back to the states on leave to marry Rosetta McBee, December 26, 1953. I had met Rosetta while we were both students at West Virginia University.

After my wife completed her degree requirements, she joined me in France. Shortly thereafter she became pregnant with our first child. Prior to the baby's arrival in November 1954, Rosetta came down with viral pneumonia and was hospitalized. In November, Rosetta gave birth to Julia Marie. She was born with spinal bifida and after two and half months she passed away in a hospital in Germany. She was a beautiful child but the abnormities were too much to overcome. Many people will say that Army people are cold and calculated, but I can tell you it is not the case. When word got out that my daughter was born with a birth defect and had to be air evacuated to Germany, General Gallagher dispatched his private plane to fly me there with the baby on my lap in an incubator. In Bordeaux, we were transferred to an air evacuation flight to Frankfort, Germany. From Frankfort, the baby and I were taken to the Ninety-Eight General Hospital in a helicopter. While back in France I had to leave for the United States on emergency leave to see my sick mother and Rosetta remained in France. While I was gone our baby passed away. Rosetta had to travel from France to Germany claim and accompany the baby back to the United States. What a nightmarish experience for all of us. Years later, I cultivated a friendship with person by the name of Bob Curran. Bob taught at Manatee, a college in our junior college league, and was a former Army major. I was telling him the details of my baby's evacuation when he interrupted me and gave the remaining details. I asked him how he knew. His told me he knew because he was the officer that worked for General Gallagher and made all the arrangements. What a small world!

This tragic event happened during our first year and half of marriage. Such adversity has a way of bringing a young couple closer together. It certainly was the case with Rosetta and me. In the ensuing years we had five beautiful and healthy children. In the fifty-five years we have been married, all of our children have brought great joy to our lives.

Summary of Ways in Which All Experiences May Help Your Career

(1) Make the best of all situations.
(2) Have a strong faith in your ability.
(3) Always consider your glass half full rather than half empty.
(4) God will always open doors and opportunities for you. Keep the faith!
(5) Meet problems and or projects with a positive attitude.
(6) Reach for the golden ring.
(7) Think, plan, and act big.
(8) Dreams become realities only when you work with a passion.
(9) Surround yourself with quality people that have the ability to take your job.
(10) Vicissitudes of life can be burdensome but never allow them to defeat you.

Chapter 3

Securing a Position – Being in the Right Place at the Right Time: From Coaching In the Army to Miami Dade Community College

Securing a position can be a very demoralizing experience to say the least. This is so since many positions require previous experience. It makes one wonder how to get this experience if those doing the hiring never give the neophyte the opportunity to prove their worth. Getting some germane experience is very important even if the experience is on a voluntary basis. This is particularly helpful if this experience is under a well respected person in your field of endeavor. Having someone of respect speak on your behalf is extremely beneficial. This all ties in with being in the right place at the right time. The key is that when a **window of opportunity** comes along you must recognize it and take advantage of that opportunity.

The Road from the Army to a College Position

While my military career was winding down, I made plans to attend graduate school. I applied for a graduate assistantship at West

Virginia University. As an undergraduate at West Virginia, I became quite close to Dr. Peter Yost who became my mentor. In fact, Dr. Yost had recommended me as a paid instructor to teach a course in Life Saving in The School of Physical Education at West University while still an undergraduate student. In light of this experience, I was offered a graduate assistantship to West Virginia University to begin once I left the Army.

An Ivy League Experience at Columbia University

Since my greater interest was to coach, I started to explore a coaching graduate assistantship rather than a teaching assistantship. A close high school football teammate of mine, Frank Vitale, was an Assistant Coach at Columbia University in New York. I mentioned to him that I was interested in coaching football on the college level while pursuing a graduate degree. Ironically, Lou Little, the well respected Head Football Coach at Columbia University, was looking for an Assistant Backfield Coach. I wasn't certain that I would be seriously considered since I had a rather lackluster college career. Frank talked to Coach Little and mentioned my experience as a very successful football coach while in the service. Coach Little became interested and requested that I send him my vita and call for an interview.

After my interview, he offered me the position as an assistant coach. Since Columbia University did not have graduate assistantships, I subsequently applied and was accepted to Teachers College of Columbia University. I was able to utilize my GI Bill of Rights to eventually receive my Masters and Doctoral degrees.

My experiences on the football staff at Columbia University were very enjoyable and helped me a great deal in my future coaching career. Back in the late fifties, the NCAA allowed two coaches to scout your next opponent three times prior to your scheduled game (presently, the teams exchange films).Being the youngest coaches on the staff, Frank Vitale and I always received the big games. One of the more memorable games was the Army-Syracuse game at West Point. I had just gotten out of the Army and not having too much money, my wife Rosetta went shopping for some suits for me at Gimbals' Bargain

Basement in New York. She bought me two beautiful suits for fifteen dollars each. They really looked *good*!

With me in a new suit, Frank and I were off to West Point for the big game. Army was still a powerhouse because they still had some quality football players following the end of the Korean conflict. As soon as we arrived at West Point, a torrential downpour struck. Being rookie coaches, we weren't wise enough to bring an umbrella or raincoat and had a long trek to the stadium. The field was a quagmire. We could hardly see the field through the rain. Syracuse won the coin toss and elected to receive. I remember thinking, why isn't Coach Schwartzwalder kicking off in light of the field's condition? That is usually common practice when the field is in such awful shape.

After they received the ball, however, Syracuse kept handing the ball off to their big running back and they moved 80 yards down the field for a touchdown. They missed the extra point, probably because the ball was too slick and the field too muddy, and four quarters later, the game ended with Syracuse winning 6-0. The running back that plowed his way down the field was Jimmy Brown! I guess Coach Ben Schwartzwalder knew his personnel well. So the moral of the story is you shouldn't be a grandstand coach!

The best part of the affair though, was that by the time I arrived home the "bargain basement" suit I was wearing dried up and shrunk! The arms of the jacket shrunk up to half way between my wrists and elbows and the pants legs shrunk up half way between my ankles and knees. My wife said I looked like Little Lord Fontroy. The next day, Coach Little asked me how the weather was at West Point. I told him it rained so hard, I ruined my suit. I didn't have the heart to tell him when he asked what my wife paid for the suit because I was embarrassed to say the least.

The Navy-Duke game at Municipal Stadium in Baltimore is another game I remember. This game was a big television game and was sold out. Sonny Jorgenson was the quarterback for Duke and George Welsh was the quarterback for Navy. The scouts from the colleges scheduled to play either Duke or Navy the next week are suppose to be guaranteed a place in the press box. Unfortunately, they ran out of room and wanted to put me and Frank in the stands. That was not acceptable because we needed a table in front of us to lay out our charts.

The press attendant decided to put us in with Harry Wismer who was doing the radio broadcast. My responsibility was to chart the backfield plays, flow in backfield, and pass routes. Frank was to chart the splits in the line and the blocking. After we got back to the hotel or home we would then synthesize the reports. In other words, the line blocking would have to match up with the backfield play. The plays would be numbered consecutively on Frank's chart and my chart. Having to chart plays in the same room with the radio announcer made it very difficult. For example, he would announce a dive play or end run as going off the left side where as the play would actually go off the right side. That night when we were putting the report together, we did quite well on the first seventy- four plays. Frank's blocking charts matched up well with my backfield charts. When we got to play seventy-five our charts didn't coincide. Frank had blocking for a play going to the left and I had a play going to right. That meant that every play after the seventy-fifth play was not correct. We worked until five in the morning trying to salvage a bad situation. I finally suggested to Frank we make the rest of the plays match up and complete the report. He said we couldn't do that because he had to give the final report to the entire staff and he couldn't lie. I was hoping Frank would be more realistic in light of our chances of beating Navy the following week. Navy ended up beating us fifty to zero! They scored all fifty points in the first half and decided not to pass the football during the entire second half. We played them real tough the second half with an eleven man front!

I learned some good lessons about over coaching versus under coaching during my experience at Columbia. One day, we were having passing drills. Coach Paul Governalli was running our pass offense against our defensive unit. I was standing in the middle of the defense to make certain our receivers were running the correct routes. One of the defensive backs came up to me and mentioned that defensive coach Stansyck told him to face the sideline when on defense and Coach Governalli told him have his back to the sideline. The player said he was confused and didn't know what to do. He wanted to know if I had any suggestions. I told him, "To be honest with you, I don't care if you stand on your head just don't allow the person you are covering to get behind you". On the following play, the player didn't stand on his head but he intercepted the next pass thrown his way. The lesson to be learned is **keep it simple, stupid (KISS).**

Working for Lou Little was a great learning experience for me. He had great rapport with the media. Two incidents made this quite clear to me. Both stories involve Stan Woodward, who during the forties and fifties was a highly respected reporter with Sports Illustrated. Frank Vitale and I were scouting the Princeton – Pennsylvania game in New Jersey. The stadium at Princeton University did not have an elevator to take the media people and coaches up to the press box. As we were starting up the high stairs, I noticed Mr. Woodward with his portable typewriter, at his advanced age, really struggling up the stairs. I approached him and said, "Mr. Woodward, can I carry that to the press box for you?"

"What's your name and where do you work?" he asked me.

I gave him my name and mentioned that I worked for Lou Little of Columbia University. The next Monday he called Lou Little and said I helped him out at Princeton. Lou called me into his office and told me how happy he was that I had the altruism and foresight to help someone in the media. He again reminded me that media people have a job to perform just like we do and that we should always respect them for that.

Another story that indicates Lou's genius in dealing with the media personnel happened during our pre-season work-outs in Lakeside, Connecticut. All the coaches had finished lunch, which consisted of a small steak and potatoes. We were sitting around the table in idle chatter when Stan Woodward walked in. Lou immediately invited him to sit down with the coaches. He asked Mr. Woodward if he had eaten. Stan said he hadn't so Lou called over Red Romo, the head trainer, who was in charge of managing the dining hall. Lou said, "Red, get my good friend Stan a nice thick steak," and showed Red his thumb and index finger spread an inch apart.

All the coaches were wondering how the cook could come up with a steak that thick. After all we hadn't had a steak thicker than one eighth of an inch! Red Romo came out with a steak the same thickness as the one we just finished eating. He laid the dish in front of Mr. Woodward and when Lou saw that scrawny steak, he told Red, in no uncertain terms, to take it back and get his good friend a thicker steak.

The coaches around the table were really feeling uneasy since we knew the nearest meat market had to be at least fifty miles away. We kept wondering how Red was going to handle this dilemma. About fifteen minutes later Red came out with an inch thick steak and put it in front of Stan. Lou couldn't say enough nice things to Red for doing this. The rest of us were really puzzled as to how Red came up with the awesome steak. We soon found out when Mr. Woodward started to cut into the steak. Red, in collaboration with the cook, decided that the only possible way they could come up with the requested thick steak was to put four or five of the steaks on hand on top of each other and place tooth picks in each corner! This story only reinforced Lou Little's desire to stay on the good side of the media!

The coaching staff at Columbia, 1955- I am bottom left. Lou Little is center. Frank Vitale is third from the right. Photo: Courtesy of Columbia University

Coaching in West "By God" Virginia

With Lou Little's retirement imminent, I started to look at the possibility of securing another position. Frank Vitale followed Paul Governalli out to San Diego State, where he became the head football coach. Since both of my parents were aging and not in good health, I thought it best that I secure a position closer to their home in New Jersey.

After applying for several positions, I accepted a position at Valley High School in Masontown, West Virginia for the 1956-1957 school year. My official title was Director of Athletics and Head Coach in Football, Basketball, and Baseball. The principal of the school, Homer Hogue, could have added custodian, disciplinarian, recreation leader, and cafeteria supervisor to my job description! What a formidable task I had before me. With this noteworthy job title, my salary, with a master's degree, was $2,800! What a step back in my career. My wife & I had one daughter, Rosemarie, and one more on the way. Our son Paul was to be born on August 29, 1957. I was given a big break when I was able to rent the second biggest house in town for $45.00 per month. The house was across the street from the mayor who had the biggest house. This big break was to become a back breaker, though, because it took about a ton of coal each week to heat the house! Luckily, one of my football players, Richard Krynicki, had an older brother who delivered a ton of coal a week for $6. The fact that I didn't know how to bank the fire at night was probably what caused us to need that much coal a week, though. I never did learn how to bank the fire so any protracted period away from the house caused the fire to burn out. Many nights my wife, daughter, and I had to go to sleep in our top coats and snow suits! At times I felt that I was a full time custodian taking care of the heating system and a part time coach.

Besides my heating problems, there were some very formidable tasks facing me at school. The Masontown High School and Arthurdale High School, bitter rivals in Preston County, became merged into Valley High School. Masontown had not won a single football game the year before and Arthurdale had only a six man football team. Needless to say, I had quite a job getting these players from divergent backgrounds to bond with each other. Arturdale was more of a white collar town and Masontown a blue collar community. In addition, I had to build up their confidence. When I met with the players from Masontown, who lost 55-0 to Barrackville High School the year before, told me Barrackville had several players who were great athletes. They mentioned that the Guin brothers were outstanding. We were scheduled to open with Barrackville at home in three weeks!

We started football workouts shortly after arriving in town. We didn't have enough quality players to have a full team scrimmage, so we only worked one half of the line against the other. With a lot of hard work and daily prayer, we were ready for our first game. As a positive coach, I had the players believe they could play against anyone. I kept stressing to our players that our opponents, regardless of how big and good they might be, put on their uniforms just like we do.

Before the game, since we didn't have a trainer or a training room, I was taping the ankles of our starting quarterback, Bill Hawley. We were using a table in the main area of the gymnasium. I was wearing a shirt and tie with-out a tie clasp while taping one of Bill's ankle. The Barrackville team came into the gymnasium on their way to the visiting team dressing room. Leading the pack was an African-American individual about 6' 4" and weighing 240 pounds. Still taping Bill's ankle, I asked, "Does Barrackville have a black coach?"

Bill said, "No coach, that's that Curtis Guin that plays fullback for them."

I was so awed by the size of Guin that I taped my tie to Bill's ankle. It was not easy to get my tie free from the tape, and on top of that, I had to convince my players all over again that they could play with these people.

Little Valley High School, in front of a sell out crowd of a thousand people, led Barrackville 19-14 with forty-eight seconds to go in the game. With our players worn down, they gave the ball to Curtis Guin and he ran about twenty yards for a touchdown after he had driven them the length of the field. The final score was 20-19, but our principal was so happy with our performance that he treated the entire team to dinner.

Our football record for the year was four wins, three loses, and two ties. The following year the Valley High School football team won the West Virginia State Championship for small high schools. I wasn't around to enjoy their success, though, since I took a teaching job in Florida. That cold winter in West Virginia did us in, particularly because my college education didn't teach how to bank a fire. I might mention that the Valley High School's basketball and baseball teams were also very competitive during the 1956-1957 school year.

The Sunshine State Comes Calling

After a miserably cold winter in West Virginia, any position in Florida would be a welcomed change. I had applied to the Dade County School system for a teaching-coaching position. Rosetta and

The Mainieri Factor

I decided to drive down to Miami for an interview. I had a very good interview with Ted Bleier, Supervisor of Physical Education, for the Dade County School system. He said he had an opening for a physical education teacher at Palm Springs Junior High School in the city of Hialeah. Mr. Bleier indicated that football positions on the high school level were hard to secure. He suggested that I take the teaching assignment for now and once I was in the system that I could make contact with the various high schools regarding a coaching position. That sounded like a logical route to take so I accepted the position at Palm Springs Junior High School.

Palm Springs was a brand new school. Miss Catherine Moore, the principal, appointed me Chairman of the Health and Physical Education Department which consisted of six instructors! This position had a big title with little additional compensation and a tremendous amount of headaches.

I met many fine people while at Palm Springs, but I really missed coaching. I talked with Joe McNulty, Head Football Coach at Miami Southwest High School, about a position. He was a real nice person and very professional. He indicated that Harry Mallios, who was a teammate of his at the University of Miami, was his backfield coach. He encouraged me to work with his club as a volunteer and he would help me get a permanent position at a later date. I had to decline his invitation because his high school was twenty miles from my permanent work location. I would never be able to get to the scheduled work outs on time.

Next, I contacted Buff Donelli, the head coach who replaced Lou Little at Columbia University. Buff said he might be able to put me on but that the position would not pay well. I figured that I would take it since I could finish my doctorate. I still had some GI Bill eligibility left to pay for my tuition.

The Window of Opportunity Opens

Windows of opportunity appear every so often in a person's life time. It is important for a person to recognize these situations and take appropriate action. As I mentioned, I was making plans to return to Columbia University. In the spring of 1960 an article appeared in the

Miami Herald that Dade County would be opening a junior college in the Miami area. The article went on to mention that the newly formed administration would begin accepting applications for faculty and staff. The college would be particularly interested in candidates that had doctoral degrees or were close to competing them.

Since I fell into that category, I decided to apply. I received an immediate response from the newly hired Dr. Kenneth Williams who was presently the president at Central Florida Community College in Ocala, Florida. He indicated to me that I would be hearing from Dr. Jack Netcher, who was to be the Director of Health, Physical Education, and Athletics. I was informed by one of the secretaries that they had approximately one hundred and twenty applicants for three positions in my field. She gave me a 9 a.m. appointment with Dr. Netcher for a Friday in March, 1960. The appointment was to be at the Dade County Board of Public Instruction in downtown Miami.

I went to the interview with a nicer suit than the one I had ruined in Columbia. Dr. Netcher and I exchanged a few pleasantries then I asked him, "Are you the same Jack Netcher that was a three time All-State player in football, baseball, and basketball at Asbury Park High School in New Jersey?"

"Well, yes that's me," he said and asked how I knew that.

I told him I was born and raised in New Jersey and remembered reading about him. Actually, Jack Netcher and Larry Doby (the first Afro-American to play in the American League), were both from New Jersey, and they were considered to be the most outstanding athletes of the early 1940's in New Jersey.

This conversation was certainly a great setting to begin my interview. Dr. Netcher indicated that he was impressed with my resume since he was looking for someone with a doctorate or close to getting one, and someone with teaching and college coaching experience. He was interested in a person that could teach physical education, could be his Assistant Baseball Coach and Business Manager of Athletics. He asked me if I would be interested in this type of position, and I told him I was. As the interview was ending, he said he had more interviews for the rest of the day but could I come back at 4 and show him around the area where I lived so he could get a feel for the housing opportunities in the Miami area. He also said that he wanted to meet my wife if she were available to go out to eat with us. I called Rosetta about this possibility but she said, with three young children at home, she didn't think she could get a baby sitter. We decided it would be better to have Dr. Netcher over to the house for dinner if it would be alright with him. He said it would be fine. We all had a nice shrimp pasta dinner prepared by my wife.

After a beautiful evening, I drove Dr. Netcher back to the Lindsey Hopkins hotel where he was staying. Just before he got out of the car, he said he was convinced that I was the person for the position. He said he had to run it past Dr. Williams and that he would get back to me. He asked me to keep it confidential, because he had many more people from the Dade County School System that he felt obligated to interview.

The following Friday, when he came back to Miami for additional interviews, he called me on the phone and officially offered me the aforementioned position. Since the new junior college would initially be under the umbrella of the Dade County School System, my salary, with the yearly increment, would transfer with me.

Some Suggested Principles to Follow When Securing a Position

(1) Know exactly what you are getting into as it relates to the size of the school, the town, the weather, and other pertinent information.
(2) It is wise to take a position that is a move up in salary and/or educational level or a lateral move. Example: Going from high school to college or college to college.
(3) Realize that you have to start somewhere. Some of the more ideal positions are not readily available.
(4) Networking is very important in securing a position.
(5) Your references should be reputable and well known to people in your field. Character references may be an exception to this principle.
(6) Prepare for the interview by doing some research on the school and/ or college. In addition, know something about the personnel you will be working with and or will be

interviewing you.

(7) Prepare a well written vita and cover letter. Have someone proof read your work. Be brief but give examples of past experiences that are related to the position you are seeking.

(8) Be confident but not over bearing; however, realize your vita and cover letter may be your only chance to show the employer why you are the person that they want to hire. These points are very important in order to be seriously considered and ultimately receive an interview.

Note: Later in this chapter, you will learn more specifically how these principles are so important to being hired.

Chapter 4

Building a Successful Program: The Miami Dade Community College Story

I REPORTED TO MIAMI DADE in August 1960. The college was being housed temporarily at Miami Central High School. During the registration of students, the Miami area was hit with hurricane Donna. This was an interesting start to my career at Miami Dade, but eventually, after some delays, we got everything rolling. Dr. Kenneth Williams was the president.

The Changing of the Guard

In early November, Dr. Netcher informed me that he was being promoted to Dean of Administration, officially effective January 1, 1961. He said I was to unofficially assume his position immediately!

From that point on, I had to plan for our inaugural baseball season without a baseball field or a single player, plan our physical education and athletic facilities, interview and hire additional professional, clerical, and support staff. In addition, I had to plan for our opening game in basketball which necessitated the hiring of game officials, plan for a concessions operation and other game management requirements. These are the kinds of challenges that come with opportunity, however. These are the kinds of challenges you should want.

Dr. Netcher said he would assist in promoting our first basketball game, because he had a tremendous amount of experience in promotions. I certainly didn't have that kind of expertise, so I welcomed his suggestions. His first suggestion related to ordering items for the concession stand. He recommended that we order five hundred pounds of shelled peanuts, a large number of soft drinks, candy, pop corn and other goodies. I said to him that the Miami area was a strong football town and that basketball did not draw well, so I was wary of ordering so much food for the concessions. He waved that away and assured me he always drew with his promotions.

He planned to send out letters to all the businesses, schools, and other organizations inviting them to our basketball opener. One of his more successful promotions was that children under twelve would be admitted free with a paying adult. A couple hundred were sent complimentary passes. Dr. Netcher had me really primed and ready for the onslaught of fans. Our team, under Coach Jim Harley, won a very exciting game. Unfortunately, other than the players of the both teams, the coaches and their wives, the crowd was well under what Jack Netcher had expected. He had his first bust as a promoter! We had enough peanuts, soda, candy, and popcorn left over to feed thousands!

One funny story emerged from this fiasco that bears telling. One day, Jack and I each took a hand full of peanuts while we headed to the men's room. While in the men's room, Jack offered one of our quite old professors some peanuts. His name was Professor Allison and he was close to retirement age. He obliged and took one of the shelled peanuts and with his arthritic hands, struggled with cracking open the shell. He finally succeeded and the nut fell out and rolled over to the edge of the urinal. The professor was so determined to get that nut that he was on his knees trying to pick it up. Dr. Netcher tapped him on the back and said, "Professor get off your knees and come back to my office. I'll give you a whole bag of peanuts from the five hundred pounds I have in the closet."

Professor Allison made frequent visits to our office for peanuts, but it took a long time to finish them off! The moral of the story is to be realistic in estimating potential crowds for athletic events.

Intercollegiate Athletics as an Integral Component of Academia

It is imperative that you, as an educator first and foremost, interpret the role of intercollegiate athletics in the broad spectrum of education. You speak in educational terms so that academicians understand the legitimate role that athletics play in the whole scheme of education. It can not and must not be mutually exclusive but must be in juxtaposition to other areas of the college curriculum. In specific terms, athletics is a form of expression and or experiences for the gifted physical education student. This is analogous to providing advanced experiences in Chemistry and Zoology and the like for the talented and gifted science students. Some of these important experiences may be nurtured and developed outside of the formal classroom setting with the athletic fields being the laboratory for students who have talented motor skills. This is no different from chemistry students experimenting in the laboratory with the skills and principles they learned in the classroom. In other words, intercollegiate athletics should never be considered extracurricular but rather an integral component of the college experience. Some other good analogies are the college newspaper and year book being a worthwhile laboratory for students majoring in journalism and English. Certainly the Debate team is a logical laboratory for speech students to hone the skills learned in the classroom.

Unfortunately, the big time athletics make this philosophy look like unrealistic dreaming, but there is no question that intercollegiate athletics has a legitimate role as healthy entertainment for students, alumni, faculty, staff, and community. This is particularly so when the programs stay within total framework of the collegiate mission. Studies by many noteworthy foundations have attempted to bring college athletics and academics closer. They have made many concrete recommendations to the various collegiate governing authorities. Many of these recommendations have already been implemented. Entrance requirements for athletes have been raised. Athletic dormitories are a thing of the past. Graduation rates among student athletes have been encouraged. These are only a few examples of the ever changing role of intercollegiate athletics. Change sometimes takes time, but it appears that the powers to be are making a concerted effort to improve the collegiate experience for all concerned.

This brief overview of intercollegiate athletics was necessary to better understand how the athletics program at Miami Dade Community College was developed. It should be quite informative to young aspiring coaches to note how and why athletics is so important to young people with physical skills.

This philosophy was the basis I used in organizing and developing the athletics program at Miami Dade Community College. My first concern was to develop a budget for the entire athletic program. Salaries for the coaches and support people came from the general tax supported fund. Construction of facilities came from tax money allocated by the state. For example, we built our gymnasium with state tax money by calling it a health center because it was used for health and physical education classes, because the state of Florida would not appropriate tax money for athletic facilities. The operational budget for the athletic program came from student activity fees. These monies would cover athletic travel, uniforms, and supplies and equipment not related to the instructional program.

Even though I reported to the president on athletic matters, I had to submit my athletic and intramural budget to the Dean of Student Affairs and, as a courtesy to the Dean of Academic Affairs, Gordon Pyle. My first athletics/intramural budget was around $70,000 which was quite modest since it covered the start up of two sports and an expanded intramural program. The Academic Dean didn't agree. He thought it was too high and wanted to know if my coaches could sell candy and doughnuts to augment the athletic budget. My answer to Dr. Pyle was that I would be happy to have my coaches on the street corners doing this if he would have his chemistry professors next to my coaches selling candy and doughnuts so they could buy test tubes for their gifted chemistry students. I explained to him that our athletic teams would be an integral part of our academics and if they had to sell candy on street corners, it would be to provide laboratory experiences for gifted physical education students. It would appear that, if this were the case, academic professors should have to do the same for their students. My budget was approved and the philosophy outlined above was the beginning of a wonderful relationship between athletics and academia.

Before I begin to explain in some detail how the Miami Dade Community College baseball program was developed, it is imperative that I describe a brief encounter I had with our new president. Our first president Dr. Ken Williams, after two years, left to take the position of president of Florida Atlantic University in Boca Raton, Florida. Our new president Dr. Peter Masiko was hired in 1963. He came to Miami after a very successful career as president of the junior system in Chicago. I did some research on him and found out that he was a very brilliant man. He graduated from Lehigh University and was a Phi Beta Kappa. He received his doctoral degree from the University of Chicago. But he was not a great promoter of athletics. I thought maybe his feelings regarding athletics was the result of receiving advanced degrees from institutions that de-emphasized intercollegiate athletics. In time, we would find out his feelings on the subject.

I was walking around campus the first day of registration when a person stopped and asked me directions to the building where registration was taking place. I gave him the directions, but before he moved on, he shook my hand and introduced himself as the new president, Dr. Peter Masiko. He asked me if I worked at the College. I answered him that I was the Director of Physical Education and Athletics and Head Baseball Coach. He said he was happy to meet me, but gave me a parting comment that was something to the effect of "I've never had much respect for physical education and athletics people."

Wow! What a first meeting with the new president. I was shocked, but I felt that I had to respond. I replied to him, "Dr. Masiko, I don't know why you have such a low regard for all of us in athletics, but I'm going to make you a believer in us."

He told me he'd never had anyone in athletics say something like that to him and delivered.

In 1966, Dr. Masiko was presenting me with a plaque designating me as a Distinguished Service Professor in front of the whole college, and he introduced me as the first person that ever pointed a finger at him and got away with it. By being positive, up beat, and a hard worker, I was the first person that finally made him a true believer in intercollegiate athletics.

Here is another experience with Dr. Masiko that laid the ground work for the relationship I would have with him. I had prepared a paper on the need for a Faculty Athletic Advisory Committee. Actually the governing body of the junior colleges (NJCCA) did not require having such a committee. I, nevertheless, sent the paper to Dr. Masiko. The original paper was sent back to me and he had written on it, "This is a well written paper, but, you have been hired as our expert in this area. If you screw up it will be your ass." It was clear to me that I was going be totally responsible for the athletic program.

The pages that follow will give you a better idea on how Dr. Masiko was converted. Hopefully, this information will give worthwhile suggestions on how to deal and relate with academicians.

A Change of Venue:
The Building of a Permanent Campus

In 1963, our permanent main campus was being developed on the abandoned Masters Field, a naval air station, in the northern part of Dade County. Prior to this move, Miami Dade Community College's North Campus had a temporary location on the Miami Central High School property. Since we were still a racially segregated college, Miami Northwestern High School, an inner city black school, housed the black campus of Miami Dade. The campus was known as the Northwestern Center. I had administrative responsibilities for the physical education and athletics programs on both campuses.

It is essential that you have some understanding on how the Miami Dade Community College developed under Dr. Masiko's leadership. Dr. Masiko made it known early on that he would move very quickly to integrate the College.

I had hired two African-Americans, both highly recommended by Dr. Oscar Moore of Florida A&M University, to teach and coach the men's and women's basketball teams. Both Carrie Meek and Ray Thornton, who had been working for sometime at Florida A&M

The Mainieri Factor

and Bethune Cookman, did a very outstanding job at Northwestern Center.

It was quite apparent that I had some difficult decisions to make. The Dean of Academic Studies called me to his office and informed me that I was to leave Carrie Meek and Ray Thornton at Miami Northwestern High School. He felt this was easy to accomplish since, at that time, we were still under the Dade County Board of Public Instruction. I informed the Dean that I absolutely could not go along with this plan. I felt that I had hired them as college teachers, and that in clear conscience, could not agree. He ordered me to follow the plan or else I was going to be relieved of my administrative duties. Since I felt so strongly about the stand I was taking, I refused to back off. For the first and only time in my career, I was insubordinate. I mentioned to the Dean that we should go in to see Dr. Masiko and get his feeling on this request. The Dean reluctantly agreed to meet with the President. I realized this was a great risk I was taking with my career, but I felt that I had no other choice. I could never live with myself if I didn't take that route. We met with the President and he felt very strongly, as I did, that we should give these faculty members every opportunity to work along with the rest of the faculty.

At my retirement banquet- Left to Right: Me, Kendrick Meek, and Carrie Meek.
– Photo: Courtesy of Bob Bailey, MD Media Dept.

Carrie Meek did an outstanding job as a noteworthy member of our faculty. After a couple more years in our area, she was promoted to Associate Dean of Community Services. Carrie then had an illustrious career in politics as a Florida Representative and as a member of the United States Congress. Many times, over the years, she mentioned to me that she speculated as to what path her career might have taken had she been forced to remain at Miami Northwestern High School. It really makes you wonder.

Ray Thornton's career was abbreviated at Miami Dade when he accepted a very well paying position with the Dade County Public Health Department. To this day both Carrie and Ray remain my close friends.

With our movement to our permanent new campus and a diversified faculty, staff and student body, it was now time to develop the necessary physical education and athletic facilities to compete on the national level. The administration gave me the responsibility, along with my staff, to develop a comprehensive physical education and athletic plan. In working with the architects, we converted the naval airplane hanger into a 5000 seat arena that would be used by the area high schools and the College. It was named the John F. Kennedy Health Center. The building provided equipment rooms, locker rooms, and offices. In addition, the old Navy Officer's club was converted into a multi purpose building with a training room, wellness and fitness center, dance studio, media room, and additional equipment and locker rooms.

DEMIE MAINIERI FIELD
-- HOME OF THE --
MIAMI-DADE NORTH FALCONS

We developed a baseball complex with two full baseball diamonds, six batting cages, dugouts, scoreboard, and stands to accommodate 3000 spectators. The baseball diamonds were to be used by the area high schools besides the college. The baseball fields were enclosed by fencing and Australian pine trees that eventually grew one hundred feet high. The College, in cooperation with the Florida Power and Light Company and the local electrical unions, installed a first class lighting system in 1969. The system had concrete polls and under ground wiring. We built a softball field that was fenced, had dugouts, bleachers, and a scoreboard. The pool and diving well came at a later date once I convinced my President that we desperately needed a pool to meet the needs, not only of the College, but the community at large. I had developed a research paper that showed the number of people that drowned in the Colleges' service area. The research also showed that there was a lack of private and public pools to serve the population of the target area. The research was so convincing that Dr. Masiko and his staff could not turn me down.

Starting a College Baseball Program from Scratch

When we started our baseball program in 1960-1961, we did so without any recruited players and without a field or batting tunnels. We did have some start up money for uniforms, balls, bats, catching gear, helmets, travel, meals and other required equipment. We had no paid assistant coach.

In one of my classes, a student, Stan Sanders, approached me about helping out with the baseball team. He had played professional baseball in the Phillies organization for three years before being released. He was interested in becoming a baseball coach. I was able to give him a tuition and books scholarship and hired him as a recreation assistant in our evening recreation program.

Stan did a very good job for me. In fact, he recruited Kurt Bevacqua who spent fourteen years in the major leagues after playing at Miami Dade in 1966 and 1967. We were allocated eighteen tuition and books scholarships the second year of our program. After he worked for me, I recommended Stan to Ron Fraser of the University of Miami where he worked as a part-time coach. I was able to arrange for him to teach physical education at St. Brendan's Elementary School. After finishing his baccalaureate degree at the University of Miami, I recommended him to Bob Wren, Head Baseball Coach at Ohio University. Stan eventually spent over twenty years as Head Baseball Coach at the University of Toledo. What a success story!

In our first year (1961) our record was 14-8. We lost to Manatee Community College in the Florida Junior College Championship game. In 1962, we lost to Manatee again in the State finals.

How did we have such success so quickly? During the fall of 1960, I visited Edison Park in the City of Miami to check on using their pool for our College swimming classes. The recreation director at Edison Park was Lefty Schemer. In the course of our conversation, I mentioned that I remembered watching him play for the Jersey City Giants which was the AAA affiliate of the New York Giants. I mentioned I needed some players at Miami Dade. He told me that the two best players in the last couple of years were John Stutz of Miami High School and Joe Taylor of Edison High School. Stutz was at Rollins College on a baseball scholarship but wanted to come back to Miami. Joe Taylor was on a football scholarship at Florida State University but wanted to give up football and just play baseball. I mentioned to Lefty that if they were interested in transferring, that they should talk to their respective coaches in order to get their releases. Once they got clearance they could call me and possibly transfer for the spring semester providing they were academically eligible.

In a couple of weeks, both John Stutz and Joe Taylor called and made an appointment to come in and meet with me. I was able to receive approval to give them tuition and books scholarships. These young players gave our program instant credibility.

We practiced at a variety of Miami and Hialeah city parks. Our message to the team each day was not about whether or not we were practicing, but rather where we were practicing. We practiced at a Little League field in Hialeah across the street from a Catholic elementary school. This venue lasted only one day because Stutz and Taylor broke too many windows in the school. I might add, that the nun was very nice and even mentioned that she was an avid baseball fan but she couldn't afford the cost of replacing the broken windows. I assured her that I would personally pay for the broken windows. When I delivered the check to her she thanked me and predicted that we were going to have a real good hitting team. She turned out to be a good judge of hitting prowess because we had a good hitting team. It was only our pitching that was suspect.

Besides finishing second in the State another memorable moment was the three run home run that Joe Taylor hit in our first game win against the University of Miami. (Senior colleges were allowed to play junior colleges at that time).

As a result of our initial success, we were able to attract most of the best baseball players in the South Florida area. Jerry Dorsch of Coral Gables High School was one of the big names that enrolled in our College. He was a big strong kid with tremendous power. One of his memorable home runs was against Ohio State. We were playing at Miami Field adjacent to the Miami Orange Bowl. Frank Howard of Ohio State hit a home run to put them ahead by three runs. In the last of the ninth inning, Jerry Dorsch hit a grand slam home run high into the Orange Bowl to win the game 6-5!

After finishing runner up to Manatee Community College in 1961, 1962 and third in 1963, we had our sights on bigger and better things for the baseball program.

The Making of a Champion

Prior to the 1964 season, I hired Barry Meyers on the recommendation of Danny Litwhiler, Head Baseball Coach at Michigan State University. Barry was a graduate assistant on Coach Litwhiler's staff. Coach Myers recruited a real outstanding recruit from West Virginia by the name of Frank Gongola. Frank was a strong power pitcher and third baseman.

We also recruited some very good prospects from the Miami area such as Pete Sarron, Steve Carlton, Kenny Mann, Jerry Greenside, Steve Polisar, Dave McCammon, Terry Stroemer, Dave Magnole, Ed Yarnell, Jorge Perez and Oscar Zamora.

Oscar was one of the early Cuban defectors. His father was a very successful medical doctor in Cuba who had to take a menial job until he was able to get a position in the medical field. Oscar worked in order to help with family finances and take his college classes at night. We were able to arrange employment for him with a builder that was developing the community of Palm Springs in Hialeah. His working hours were flexible so he could still attend classes and attend baseball work outs. It took some creative planning, but it worked out well. Needless to say, it took a great person like Oscar to make it work. The fact that Oscar eventually pitched in the major leagues with Houston and the Chicago Cubs only proved his determination, drive, and talent.

The Steve Carlton Saga

The Steve Carlton story is quite interesting. I had offered him a tuition and book scholarship ($300) when he graduated from North Miami High School. This offer was made in June of 1963. Steve turned me down indicating that he wanted to play professional baseball. In late August, Steve had a change of heart and contacted me. I indicated to Steve that I had committed all of my scholarship money, but he was welcome to come with us if he agreed to pay his tuition and fees and once I had some aid available, I would give him a scholarship. Steve agreed to the arrangement and pitched all fall of 1963. In December, Steve came to my office to ask for some advice regarding his career. He indicated that Chase Riddle of the St. Louis Cardinals had offered him a $5000 signing bonus. This was possible since major league baseball did not begin the free agent draft until 1966. My advice to Steve was that if he felt he wouldn't be making our rotation that it might be wise to sign. In fairness to Steve, I felt it was essential that he pitch enough innings in order to develop his potential. I told him that the final decision was his. He decided to sign and was in the major leagues by September, 1964 after winning big in the minor leagues. Miami Dade Community College won the Junior College World Series in 1964. Just possibly, had Steve stayed with us, we would have gone undefeated! In the end though, things worked out well for Steve Carlton and Miami Dade.

Steve Carlton (right) instructing Rudy Daumy, a player at Miami Dade- Photo: Courtesy of Bob Bailey MD Media Dept.

There are some other interesting incidents regarding Steve. In the spring of 1964, Eddie Stanky, Director of Player Development for the St. Louis Cardinals, invited Miami Dade to play their Rock Hill ball club at their minor league complex in Homestead. After our club roughed up a couple of the Rock Hill pitchers, the manager brought in

Steve Carlton to pitch. After the score got to 19-0, Eddie Stanky came over to me and said, "It's 5:45 PM and this skinny kid isn't going to get anyone out."

But Steve sure did get a lot of guys out to get promoted to the major leagues so quickly!

After Steve Carlton won his first Cy Young award, the City of North Miami had a Steve Carlton Day and banquet and invited me to be the feature speaker! In my introductory comments, I indicated that it was a little unusual for the banquet committee to invite me to talk about Steve Carlton and his pitching accomplishments since I was going to make him a first baseman because of his hitting prowess. I was only kidding, but the comment got around professional baseball. In fact, Don Sutton years later kidded me about the comment but always mentioned he knew what kind of pitching staff I had on that national championship team. Don, who pitched at Gulf Coast Community College, threw a three hitter against us and lost when Frank Gongola threw a no hitter against him. I might add that the people from ESPN Classic flew a person into South Bend, Indiana to interview me for the story they were doing on Steve Carlton. I was interviewed for one hour and told them this story of Steve's abbreviated college career. They never used any of the material. I was a little disappointed because this phase of Carlton's career is a powerful story. Winning four Cy Young Awards and being inducted into the Hall of Fame are monumental accomplishments. How he achieved these is truly phenomenal!

From Scratch to Champion

Winning a national title, in itself, is quite an accomplishment. Winning one, four years after starting the program, is just unbelievable. Developing a championship program takes a great deal of hard work, commitment and luck. Recruiting good players is a must. You have to be able to identify the tools necessary to play the game, but also it is very important to recruit players who have the make up and intangibles to be winners. I will go into more detail later on how you can evaluate make up. I will, at least, give you my perspective on how I evaluate this very important area. Professional scouts, coaches, recruiters, and player development people will give you a wide variety of ways in which this can be accomplished. Once we get to this in a future chapter, you will enjoy the spectrum of approaches.

Common knowledge says that you must be strong up the middle to have a winning ball club. With this in mind, you must recruit pitchers that not only throw hard but have command. You can never have too many pitchers. Our national championship team had three top quality starters in Frank Gongola, Gerry Greenside, and Oscar Zamora. Gongola was a real hard thrower with a slider that had a good bite. Greenside was crafty who had an average major league fast ball but knew how to pitch. Zamora had an above average curve ball. I might add that all three of these pitchers had unbelievable make up. They were just plain tough as nails. After winning the Junior College World Series, Oscar signed professionally and had a nice big league career with Houston and the Chicago Cubs. Gerry signed with the Phillies but did not make it to the major leagues.

Since Frank Gongola was only a freshman, he had another year with us. His story is unbelievable and sad. Frank, after the Junior College World Series, went back to West Virginia to work and stay close to home. He was the youngest of nine brothers who were all great athletes and many played professional baseball. I received a phone call from Jack Stallings, the baseball coach at Wake Forest University, who was coaching at Sturgis, South Dakota in the very prestigious college Basin League. Jack was in dire need of some pitching and inquired about Frank Gongola. I told him that Frank was back in West Virginia. He mentioned that if he was interested in playing in Sturgis, he should call him right away. I called Frank's home and his Mom said he was working as a truck driver for Armour Packing Company. I called Armour's main office in Wheeling, West Virginia to find out if I could get in touch with Frank Gongola, and they indicated that he was on a delivery somewhere between Wheeling and Charleston, West Virginia. I called the West Virginia State Police barracks in Wheeling and asked if they would be kind enough to have one of their patrol cars track down a Frank Gongola driving Armour's truck somewhere on the main highway between Wheeling and Charleston. I asked that he immediately call Coach Mainieri in Miami. I gave the officer my phone number when he honored my request. Frank agreed to fly out to South Dakota to pitch for Sturgis. Frank said "that anything beats driving a truck". Coach Stallings called me a week later and told me that Frank pitched a three hit shut out in his first outing but blew out his arm. He never pitched another game after that. He came back to Miami Dade for his sophomore year and tried to play the outfield without success. I had Frank examined by two different orthopedic surgeons who said he tore something in the shoulder but surgery was not possible. Rotator cuff surgery was not common in 1964. After Frank left Miami Dade I lost touch with him. I found out that he died years later as a homeless person. This was told to me by Dave Cisar, who came from the same town in West Virginia as Frank. Dave played for me at Miami Dade in 1965.

In order to qualify for the Junior College World Series, we had to win two out of three games against Manatee Community College. The games were played at a neutral site in Ft. Myers, Florida. Manatee won the first game, 4-2 in 12 innings. We won the second game 9-2 and the third game 9-6 in 11 innings. In that final game, we were losing 6-5 in the ninth inning with two outs and two strikes on Pete Sarron, when he singled to right field. Kenny Mann hit a long double off the left center wall scoring Sarron from first base. In the 11 inning, with the bases loaded, Frank Gongola hit a double in the same area as Mann's double in the ninth inning knocking in all three runs for a come from behind 9-6 win! I might add that Pete Sarron was the son of Petey Sarron, Featherweight Boxing Champion of the World. Just possibly, genetics is a factor in athleticism!

After beating Manatee, we traveled to Pensacola, Florida and beat Gulf Coast Community College 3-2 and 4-3. Gongola pitched a no hitter in the first game with Gulf Coast getting two unearned runs. We beat their two aces and future major league players, Don Sutton and Q. V. Lowe. Don Sutton of course, was later inducted into the Hall of Fame. One never knows, had Steve Carlton remained with our club rather than signing professionally, two future Hall of Fame inductees may have pitched against each other in those games in Pensacola.

Our last obstacle, before heading to Grand Junction, Colorado for the Junior College World Series, was a play-off against Brewton Parker of Georgia. We beat them 4-3 in the first game, ending the game with a triple play. The second game we won 4-1. Both games were played at Miami Stadium, since we didn't have our baseball facility on our campus as yet.

Since we had to immediately make plans for our trip to Colorado, I instructed my rookie Business Manager, John Moore, to come up with a dollar figure to cover our trip. Dr. Masiko had to request the funds from our Board of Trustees, so we needed the budget pronto. John came back with a figure that reflected the cost for a **one way fare** for our travel party. Dr. Masiko received approval on that budget before we noticed the honest error. Since Dr. Masiko felt very uncomfortable about going back to the board, we were forced to bus it from Miami, Florida and return. Believe me when I say we had a lot of team togetherness by the time we arrived in Grand Junction. Ken Small wrote a very derogatory article indicating that Miami Dade had to send their poor baseball team to the Junior College World Series by bus! Both Dr. Masiko and I were livid and embarrassed. Over the years, Dr. John Moore, who became an assistant athletics director at the University of South Carolina, always reminded me that the only time Miami Dade won a national championship was when we traveled by bus. Maybe Dr. Moore was correct because we were fortunate to go four more times to the Junior College World Series by air and finished runner-up three times and third once.

Reunion of my 1964 National Championship team. – Photo: Courtesy of Bob Bailey Miami Dade Media Department

Keeping the Tradition Going

Keeping the tradition going is never an easy task. This is made particularly difficult since the expectations are made high by the coaching staff, the players, the college administration, the media, and followers of the team.

With a highly set bar, we had to recruit some quality players to keep the ball going. We were able to put a pretty good club together for the 1965 season, however, we lost in the eight team tournament to Gulf Coast Community College in the championship game. The tournament was played at our new campus facility.

The game ended with one of our players, in an act of frustration, throwing his batting helmet. It accidentally hit the Gulf Coast first baseman. A lot of pushing and shoving ensued. The coaching staffs from both clubs moved quickly to avert a really bad situation. I was devastated with the action of one player, since I always preached to my players to handle winning and losing with class. We didn't lose with dignity that time. I was completely embarrassed and hurt by the way we handled the loss. When I got home that night, I told Rosetta I was disgusted by it all. I felt like retiring as coach of Miami Dade, I was hurting that much. Rosetta gave me some very good advice. She said I should sleep on the situation and then decide in the morning what to do. She also mentioned that in her opinion, retiring with a cloud over the baseball program would not be good. She thought it would be better for me to take punitive action against the player whose action was the cause of this unfortunate incident. My retiring at that point would be tantamount to being a "quitter". She was well aware that quitting under any circumstances was repugnant to me.

I remained as coach. The player who threw his helmet never played another inning for Miami Dade. He transferred to Jacksonville University. The baseball program, under my tutelage, returned to the Junior College World Series in 1966, 1967, 1971, and 1974.

Ken Small of the Miami Herald, called me during August 1965. When I answered the phone, I was greeted with, "Doc, this is Ken Small of the Miami Herald who wrote that **horse bleep** article about your 1964 club having to bus your team to the Junior College World Series in Grand Junction, Colorado".

I said, "Ken that is old stuff and I forgot about the article. What can I do for you?"

Ken said, "I am now working at the Miami Herald out of the Palm Beach Office, and I saw a pitcher who can really pitch. He is pitching in the championship game of the regional American Legion tournament. You have to come up to see him pitch because he is that good."

I informed Ken that I had already finished my recruiting.

He said, "Please come, I really want to redeem myself after that *horse bleep article*."

I told him that I would be there. After I got off the phone, I had to break the news to my wife that we would have to postpone going out to dinner that night because I would have to go see some kid pitch that had been recommended by Ken Small.

My wife's response was, "I hope Ken Small's eye for baseball talent is better than his reporting skills."

It was heart warming to find out my wife's hope about Ken Small was true, and my trip to Lake Worth to see Joe Arnold pitch vindicated him. Joe Arnold would be a great addition to our baseball program. He became instrumental in our team trips to the Junior College World Series in 1966 and 1967.

The records Joe Arnold holds at Miami Dade are unbelievable to say the least.

(1) In 1967 he started 17 games and completed 16.
(2) He holds the Miami Dade record for the most innings pitched in a season- 176 2/3 (1967); most shutouts-10 (1967); most innings pitched in the Junior College World Series-30 2/3 (1966); most strikeouts in a single season- 190 (1967) ; most wins in a single season- 18(1967) ; most wins in two seasons-29(1967&1968); best earn average- 0.40(1967).

Joe Arnold was a pleasure to watch pitch. He was always in complete command. He made things look easy. He was a two time NJCAA All-American and a NCAA All-American at Arizona State University before signing with the Houston Astros as an *infielder!*

There is no doubt that Joe Arnold continued to set the bar higher for the future Falcon teams.

We were fortunate enough to return to the Junior College World Series in 1971 and 1974. It was poetic justice that Joe Arnold returned from professional baseball to be an assistant coach on our 1974 team.

I might mention that our 1969 team had some of the best talent of any team I coached at Miami Dade. We had three future major league players on that team but lost 2-1 to Manatee Community College in fifteen innings. Manatee had four future major league players on their club that beat us. Unbelievably, the game was tied at 1-1 after 9 innings but was suspended for three days because of rain. I couldn't bring back my hard throwing pitcher Ray Bare because I didn't want to hurt his arm. Manatee brought back a soft throwing left handed pitcher by the name of Pat Osborne whom we couldn't handle. Both Pat Osborne and Ray Bare later played in the major leagues.

In Summary, my thirty years of coaching baseball at Miami Dade was a great run. Our success was the result of having great players, great facilities and administrative support. Thirty of our former players played in the major leagues, ninety were drafted or signed by professional baseball, and one hundred and forty-two received scholarships to four year colleges. These are indeed impressive numbers that may give some valid reasons for our success, but really the underlying ingredient was our unwavering passion to succeed. Maybe there was also a little luck involved but I think it was Branch Ricky who said **luck is the residue of design.**

Summary of Areas that Contribute to a Successful Program

1. Establish rapport with area youth and High School coaches, area scouts. They may give you valuable information on the prospects' tools and makeup. Talk to the opposing coaches of the players you are trying to recruit. They may give you some important information on their makeup. They may answer questions on how the player performs under pressure.
2. Develop clinics for area players and coaches.

3. Plan a "kick off" dinner to generate interest in the coming baseball season. Notre Dame has had a very successful program using this approach.
4. Build up good public relations by staging a celebrity golf tournament at an area country club. At Miami Dade, we had such a successful event at the Doral Country Club under the direction of Dr. Ron Warnock of my staff. It started out with my former players in the major leagues as the celebrities. It became such a huge success when additional major league players got involved. It was organized whereby the golf tournament was on Friday and a clinic for the area youngsters was on Saturday and Sunday. Joe DiMaggio and Tom Lasorda were some of our keynote speakers.

The left picture of me, Don Shula, and Tommy Lasorda is from the first celebrity golf tournament at Doral.

The picture of me and Joe DiMaggio is from the kids' clinic that we held in conjunction with the golf tournament.

Photo: Courtesy of Bob Bailey of MD Media Department

Chapter 5

Destiny as a Factor in Securing a Position: From Coaching at Columbus High School to the University of Notre Dame

This chapter was written by my son Paul.

Sometimes your advancement depends on you happening to be in the right place at the right time. The window of opportunity appears very infrequently, so you need to be able to recognize it when it does.

The Professional Baseball Dream

Since my dad was a long time college coach, I grew up around baseball. Every young boy that grows up playing baseball wants to be a major leaguer some day. I was no different. After my collegiate career ended, I had an opportunity to play professional baseball in the Chicago White Sox organization. But after two years in the minor leagues, despite my burning desire to play in the major leagues, I was realistic and smart enough to know that my natural talent could only take me so far.

Paul the batboy.

David Dombrowski, director of player development for the Chicago White Sox at the time, called me into his office and told me that he was releasing me and that I should consider going into coaching like my dad. He and his staff thought at best I might reach AA baseball. It seemed that being a major league baseball player did not appear to be a realistic goal.

Despite the disappointment of being released, I felt I needed to get on with my life, too, so I managed to secure a teaching position at Columbus High School in Miami, as well as assisting with the football and baseball teams.

The High School Coaching Experience

Jim Hendry, now Vice President and General Manager of the Cubs, was the head baseball coach at Columbus High School at the time. We had become great friends during the summer before my senior year in college when I played in the Cape Cod Summer League and Jim was an assistant coach for the same team. I assisted Jim with the team at Columbus and, after three years together, Jim moved on to

Creighton University as an assistant coach. He eventually became head coach and led Creighton to the College World Series in 1991.

After Jim left Columbus High School, the administration decided on another person to become the new head coach instead of me. Since I had been an athlete at Columbus High School, played professional baseball, and had been on the staff there, this was a tremendous disappointment and setback for me. The principal at Columbus wanted me to stay on the staff as an assistant. However, I declined his offer because I felt it would be an awkward situation to be an assistant for someone who I thought didn't deserve the job as much as I did. I resigned from Columbus High School because I felt it was the thing to do. Growing up in my home, my dad always stressed the importance of being loyal to the person above you. I wasn't about to be in a situation that would challenge my loyalty.

The St. Thomas University Experience

When I informed my dad of my resignation, he was very supportive of my decision. However, he was concerned that I resigned before I had another job lined up. He had always taught me to make decisions on valid principles, which I did, however, resigning from one job before having another was not a decision based on sound reasoning.

A few days later, my dad had a phone call from Ken Stibler, director of athletics at Biscayne College, the school that was to become St. Thomas. Ken told him that he was trying to locate me because he was looking for a new coach.

After talking to my dad, I called Ken Stibler and arranged an interview. During the interview, he offered me the head coaching position at Biscayne. However, before I was to be announced as the head coach, he told me I would have to find another job to supplement my pay as head coach at Biscayne. I was to make a grand total of $3200.

I decided to talk to the administration at Monsignor Pace High School regarding a teaching position. Pace was a catholic high school adjacent to Biscayne College. If I could teach there, it would be a workable situation to drive next door at the end of classes and coach in the afternoon. At Pace, I was offered the job of teaching Biology and Marine Biology. I was happy to receive the job, although I didn't know very much about Marine Biology. Balancing the two jobs turned out to be a very challenging task but I felt I was paying the price to be successful in the profession.

After the first year, Dr. Joe Hoy, chairman of the sports management curriculum at St. Thomas, hired me as an instructor. What a break! This allowed me to be on campus full time and in a better position to develop the baseball program.

Later, I was given the extra duties as Director of Athletics. Shortly after I accepted that job, however, a consultant firm was brought to study the athletics program and to determine whether or not it could continue. I spent many hours working with the consultant firm and in the end was able to convince them that a viable athletic program could exist at St. Thomas with some program modifications and creative financial support. This was good news because I could keep my employment and support my ever-growing family. I learned a very valuable lesson during this stressful time – NEVER take anything for granted!

I spent six years developing the baseball effort into a respectable winning program. We had a lot to overcome with limited scholarships and limited facilities. However, I was having a great time because I was coaching college baseball and working with young men. Prior to my taking over the program, St. Thomas had never had a winning season in baseball. We didn't win any championships there but I was proud that we became a respectable Division II college baseball program. Fifteen of my former St. Thomas players made it into professional baseball, while three made it to the major leagues.

One day at St. Thomas I received a phone call from the head baseball coach at the US Air Force Academy, wondering if they could use our field for a game against Michigan State University. I told him that was fine; they could use it for free, under one condition. I asked him to play us one game also. Little did I know how much that conversation would affect the rest of my life?

The Air Force Academy on the Horizon

The coach at Air Force agreed to the arrangement as they were thrilled to have use of our field. We played one of our better games of the year beating the Falcons 13-0. We must have fooled them as they thought we looked well coached because after the game, their coach thanked me for the use of the field and then shocked me by asking if I was interested in applying for his job at the Air Force Academy. He told me the administration was going to hire their first civilian head baseball coach. The previous coaches were all military officers that only remained on the staff for a few years at a time. The only problem was that the application deadline was three days away. I said I was interested but I didn't know how I'd apply in time. They said that was ok because they would gladly hand carry my resume to the chairman of the screening committee. They invited me to dinner later that night, where we had some pizza at their hotel. We talked, got to know each other, and they took my resume back for me. Colonel Danny Litwhiler Jr. was traveling with the club and he mentioned that he thought his dad, former baseball coach at Florida State and Michigan State knew my dad. What a small world.

Sometime in the next couple days, I ran into Don Shula on the St. Thomas campus. The Dolphins' training camp and facilities were on St. Thomas's campus. I knew Coach Shula because I had a few dealings with him in my job as athletic director at St. Thomas. He asked me what was new so I told him about the athletics situation at St. Thomas and how it was on shaky grounds, even after the consultant firm decided to retain the program.

With this in mind, I thought that I would pursue other coaching opportunities. I mentioned that I was applying to the Air Force Academy and asked if I could use him as a reference.

"I generally prefer the hiring organization to call me for a recommendation," he said, "but since I know you so well and have seen you coach first hand, I would be glad to phone the athletic director at the Academy on your behalf."

In addition to Coach Shula's recommendation, Tommy Lasorda also called on my behalf. Colonel John Clune, the athletic director at Air Force was overwhelmed by those two calls. I know he was because he told me about 100 times.

A week or so later, I received a call from Colonel Clune. He indicated that I was one of the finalists for the job. We set up a time for my wife and me to fly out to Colorado Springs for an interview.

At the interview, I was asked about how I would plan and execute a practice schedule at the Academy, where the cadets were on a very tight academic and military training program. They had a very limited number of hours to engage in intercollegiate athletics. I answered the committee's question by showing them the detailed planning system I had used while at St. Thomas. Additionally, I was interviewed by several areas of the Air Force Academy's academic and athletic community. My wife and I both loved Colorado and eventually I was offered the position.

Building a winning program at the Academy was very challenging, since the prospective players had to receive a U.S. Senate or Congressional appointment, have extremely high grades, and have a variety of school and community activities. In addition, the cadets could not play summer league baseball, as they had to intern at an Air Force base somewhere around the world during their break. Also the players had to know they were coming to a school where they could not sign a professional baseball contract because of their commitment to the service once they graduated.

They were all very dedicated players, though, who rose to the occasion and worked as hard as they could to become as good as they could be. Our teams at Air Force had the first winning seasons in nearly a decade. We averaged 26 wins a season. The 1994 squad led the nation in hitting (.360) and slugging (.623). I coached three all-Americans, two freshman all-Americans, and two Academic all-Americans.

In summary, working at a higher educational institution like the United States Air Force Academy gave me a tremendous opportunity to work with very intelligent and hard working young men. It certainly prepared me for the next stop in my career.

Baseball Under The Golden Dome

While at Air Force, we played Notre Dame one time and it came to my attention that the job there had a possibility of opening because their coach was being considered for the Arizona State position. I talked to my dad about things and told him I had an interest in the Notre Dame position should it open. He said, "Paul, don't get your hopes up."

My dad always said he wasn't a very good forecaster of the future, including things like the weather, the outcome of athletic events, and political elections. My dad's self-analysis was correct and the Notre Dame position opened up.

Apparently, someone connected with the University of Notre Dame, called Dave Dombrowski (then General Manager of the Florida Marlins), and asked him to recommend someone for the position. Dave, who watched my career following my release from the White Sox, conferred with Jim Hendry (who was working for the Marlins at the time) and ultimately recommended me for the position. You can see how all of my past experiences and all the impressions I made on people I met started to come together and affect the chances of being considered for Notre Dame.

In mid August of 1994, the athletic director at Air Force, Colonel Schweitzer, called me on the phone and said he had received a phone call from Dick Rosenthal, Director of Athletics at Notre Dame, asking for permission to speak with me about the coaching position under the Golden Dome. A few minutes later, I was on the phone with Dick Rosenthal. He said my name had repeatedly appeared as a viable candidate regarding the hiring of a new baseball coach. I told him I was very interested in the job, and he asked to come to South Bend for an interview. I told him I was in a tough spot because my wife was due to have our fourth child any day.

My wife gave birth to our second son, Thomas, on August 23, 1994. Two days later, I flew to South Bend and met with Dick Rosenthal. After meeting with several administrators and coaches, I was offered the position of head baseball coach. I resigned my position at the Air Force Academy and was introduced as the new coach at a Notre Dame press conference.

My tenure at Notre Dame has been a great challenge and an enjoyable experience. In 2002, my team earned its way to the College World Series, the programs first trip to this great event in 45 years!

The Mainieri Factor! Top: Paul and Demie at Notre Dame. Right: Paul and sons, Nick and Tommy, at Rosenblatt Stadium, Omaha, Nebraska. Bottom: Paul's son and Notre Dame Batboy Tommy being interviewed by the press at the College World Series. Two photos on top and right: Courtesy of Joe Brown

Chapter 6

Building a Power at the University of Notre Dame

This chapter was also added by my son Paul.

SOON AFTER BEING NAMED head baseball coach at Notre Dame, my dad, Tom Lasorda, Rod Dedeaux, and I were having dinner at a restaurant in Chicago. Coach Dedeaux congratulated me on my new job. Coach Dedeaux, of course, was the legendary coach of Southern Cal, where he had experienced success of which other coaches only dream.

I asked him if I would ever be able to develop the program at Notre Dame to the level of being College World Series competitive.

His answer was quite direct. "Paul, don't build your hopes up along those lines because as a northern university, you have no chance of getting to the College World Series. I don't believe you'll ever be able to do it." He wished me well in my new challenge. I love Rod, he's the greatest coach in college baseball history, and I know he didn't mean anything negative about me. However, I took that comment as a challenge to prove him wrong.

How could a person like me, who was raised and played baseball in the south and had a father who had success coaching in that climate, end up facing the task of building a quality program in the north? All I heard over the years was that the best baseball was played in warm climates. However, after a great deal of hard work, the 2002 University of Notre Dame team made it to the World Series. The following pages will give you an insight as to how it happened. When I saw Rod Dedeaux on the field before one of our games in Omaha, we gave each other a big hug and he told me how proud he was of me. That meant more to me than anything you could imagine.

Hiring a Coaching Staff

When I arrived at Notre Dame, my first challenge was to hire an assistant coach that had the potential to take my job down the road. This was following the advice Lou Little, the legendary football coach from Columbia University, gave to my dad, who then passed it on to me.

My first hire was Brian O'Connor, who had pitched for Jim Hendry at Creighton University, and was a member of that 1991 College World Series team. Brian was highly recommended by Jim and he turned out to be a gem. After working with me for nine years he was appointed head coach at the University of Virginia. He is doing great work and is becoming one of the top head coaches in the country.

My second hire was Cory Mee, who had played at Notre Dame. He was the real teacher of our staff. He was able to give me important information about Notre Dame and its organization, policies, and the like. After five years on my staff, he became the top assistant coach at Michigan State University; and then head coach at the University of Toledo.

Another assistant of mine at Notre Dame, David Grewe was appointed Head Baseball Coach at Michigan State University in the summer of 2005. This appointment was made after spending three years as an assistant at the University of Notre Dame. He is the sixth former assistant of mine who have become a head coach at a major university.

For all you coaches out there, hiring someone that could take your job one day is a good principle to follow. Before Notre Dame, it worked for me at St. Thomas, where Al Avila was one of my assistants. He is now assistant general manager for the Detroit Tigers. It also worked well for me at Air Force, where Eric Campbell became the head coach after I left for Notre Dame. He now runs the USA Baseball National team program.

You can't do it yourself. You must trust your assistant coaches and you don't want people who are "Yes Men" either. Learn to delegate and hold your coaches accountable, however. You have to be on the same page philosophically. When you leave the office after a staff meeting, you must be a united front to the players. There is no substitute for absolute loyalty— in both directions! You're all in it together! As a wise man once said, it's amazing what can be accomplished when no one cares who gets the credit.

Administrative Support

Getting the support of the administration is also equally important. When I arrived at Notre Dame, they already had the beautiful Frank Eck Stadium. Once I evaluated the facilities, I deciphered what we needed to make the baseball plant better. After having a successful few seasons, an indoor batting and pitching facility was added, something crucial when you are a northern school competing with the big southern programs. The facility has clay mounds that help our pitchers get ready for our spring trips. In addition, the outdoor batting cages were upgraded. We still had access to the Loftus Center, Notre Dame's large indoor facility designed for football, where we are able to take infield and outfield practice.

Administrators have a tough job providing financial support to all the different sports. I was an athletic director at St. Thomas, so I knew how to work with the administration. Above all, winning games helps to get them on your side. Staying realistic and reasonable also helps to maintain rapport with athletic administrators.

Putting a Schedule Together

Being able to develop an attractive spring schedule, which includes trips to warm weather schools, is a must. It takes money, but it is necessary to get your club ready for the conference schedule.

The more you play against the traditionally great programs, the less intimidated you become of them. I tell our players to respect all our opponents, but be in awe of no one. Therefore, we try to schedule challenging games. However, if every game at the start of the year is against a top team, your team could become demoralized. I feel comfortable playing anybody on a neutral field or in a tournament format, but I rarely want to take on a top-ranked team in a three-game series in their park at the beginning of the season. It is our first time outside and they've already played fifteen games – a tremendous advantage. You must be smart and have a balance in your schedule. Remember, success builds greater confidence.

Recruiting, Recruiting, and Recruiting!

It takes the proper resources in order to recruit on the national basis. This is particularly true at Notre Dame because we have such high academic standards. We scour the country for the most talented players who also have the academic potential to succeed at Notre Dame. We are proud of being able to attract quality student-athletes. This is reflected in the fact that our Notre Dame teams have combined for a 100% graduation rate among players who have completed their eligibility. The ten who signed professionally after their junior year have returned to complete or are in the process of completing their degree requirements. It is a must to have the players with talent, and equally important, players with the right attitude toward the game and academics.

Find the right fits for your program. For us, we need to recruit a lot of players that are used to cold weather. You can then sprinkle in some players from more warm weather areas that have played a lot of baseball and have great instincts. Many of our players from the warm areas who have done well for us were not necessarily the top level individuals from those places. However, they had the right attitude to come north and believed in the school and the coaches.

Our best class ever was the group that eventually took us to the College World Series. Not one of those players was drafted out of high school. Six were from the north and three were from warm weather areas. Five of them signed professionally after completing their college eligibility.

You need to be strong on the mound. We spend about 50% of our scholarship money on pitchers. We spend about 40% on catchers and middle infielders. Athletes who are versatile allow us to refrain from recruiting many position players. I try to get players that are "gamers" and do well in the clutch. Sometimes I recruit a player because they showed how they handle failure in the game.

Practice Organization- What We Want to Accomplish

Indoor workouts are awful. I don't like them. Also inside, I get concerned that our players become good at doing drills - at the expense of losing their instincts for the game. Therefore, as radical as it sounds, sometimes I feel that less coaching is better during indoor drills.

We make getting their throwing arms and legs in shape a top priority. Pitchers throw in competitive situations in the tunnels and hitters get at bats off of them. Our outfielders do very little defensively indoors because there isn't very much they can do. Our infielders do what we call "glove drills" just to handle the ball more often. We play a lot of pepper indoors and have throwing relay races, just to get the kids to handle the ball as much as they can. Our practices indoors are very short. We don't want our players to get cabin fever.

We place a huge importance on fall practice. Not only is this our instruction time, it is our time to find out which players are going to fit into the lineup in the spring. We play a scrimmage game every single day of fall practice. Some days this game may be only three innings, others as many as eight. By doing this and stopping frequently to make coaching points regarding base running or cut offs and the like, our players apply the fundamentals to real game situations.

My hope is that those instincts will return to the player quickly once we get outside in the spring. Most of the time in the spring we will practice only one day outdoors before our first game, sometimes not at all!

It's All a State of Mind

I am not a sports psychologist, so I am not going to write as detailed as one would, but I need to tell you in general terms how your attitude and the players' attitudes are prerequisites for where your program will go.

As coaches, you can't accept excuses from your players. It is my practice that our coaches not make excuses as to why we can't be successful because the players will use them, too. Take your team and say, "These are the cards we have been dealt; now we have to roll up our sleeves and go to work. What the mind believes, the body achieves! Winning is a state of mind." We encourage our players to actively visualize successful turns at bat and in the field. Negative thoughts are anathema to success.

Every year is a new year. We must remember what got us to this point, as the new season doesn't pick up where the last one ended. Establish realistic expectations for your team. Make players feel great about what they have accomplished. I always felt that if players were sad to see the season end, I did my job. Create a positive environment with expectations. In the end, celebration dog piles are the culmination of the efforts of many people. Only one team will finish the season with a win. Don't let your last game determine the worth of your program. We came up short a number of times at Notre Dame and finally got over the hump, making the World Series in 2002. In the end, all you have is memories! Make them good memories for the players.

Team Building

Everyone knows we don't over-recruit. We stick with the players and let them play through their slumps. It may be somewhat of a gamble and we may end up short in an area, but you need to stick with the guys you've got. It's the only way to instill confidence in them. Believe it or not, it is a positive to not have too many players. If we had an abundance of players, some coaches would probably act like a yo-yo. In other words, in one day and out the next! Develop a role for everyone. They may not be happy with their role but be up front and honest with them. I know they will appreciate this. Talk frequently with individual players. Determine who the leaders of your team will be and really help guide them. Do a lot of things that build leadership and allow the players to be involved in many aspects of your program. Very often we will tell them our rationale for doing things and, by not keeping them in the dark; they will buy into what the coaches believe.

Feel Good about Being a Leader

Don't let getting to the World Series be your gauge for success. That will only lead to frustration for everyone. All those years we came close, I never felt frustrated, nor did we let the players feel like failures.

Coach for the right reason - to help young people! Make it your goal that the players develop their talent to the fullest and enjoy the experience. If you recruit good enough players, you will experience success commensurate with your talent. We appreciate all the compliments that people have given us, since we sense many people are amazed that a northern school like Notre Dame made it to the World Series. However, we haven't done anything differently now than we did at Air Force, when we were fortunate to win as many games as we lost during a season. The same was true at St. Thomas University. The only difference is that we are now at a place that can attract a higher level of player. We have had to make some adjustments because of the weather, but there are a lot more important things than that! Wherever you coach, it would be my advice to recruit good players, work hard to maximize the potential of your program, create a positive atmosphere on your team, and enjoy the journey!

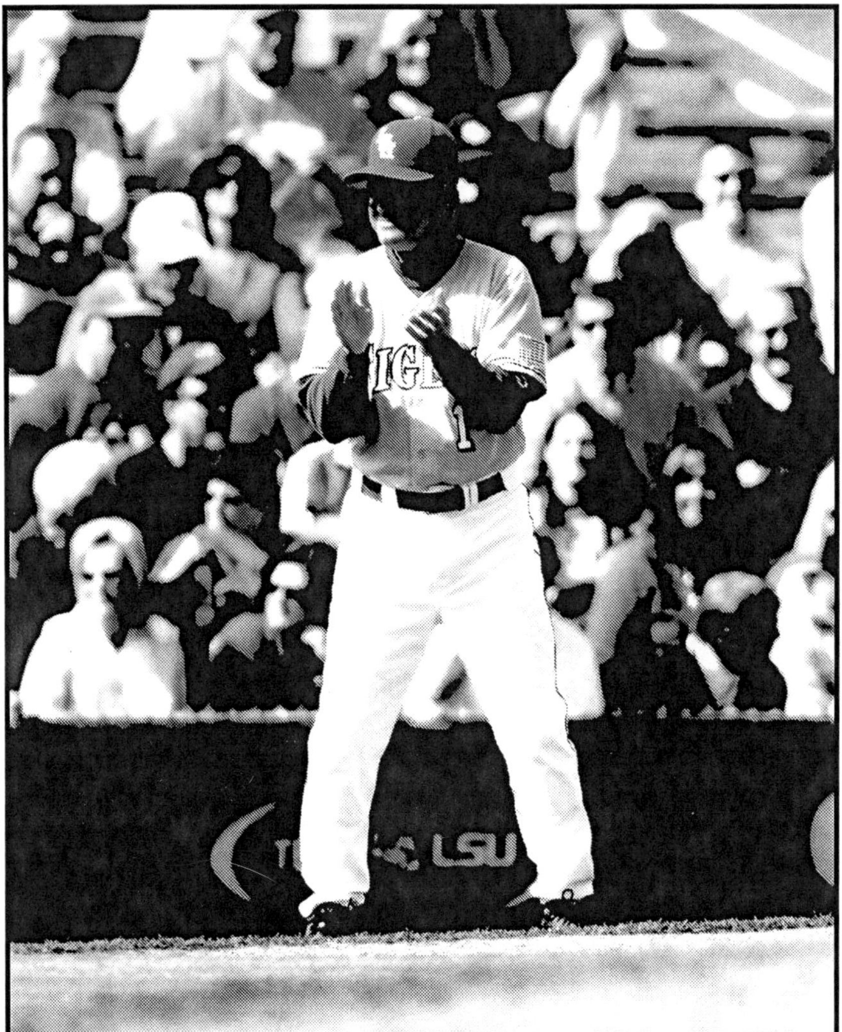
LSU

Chapter 7

A Potpourri of Stories

The majority of these stories come from my coaching career, while the ones at the end come from my son Paul's and are told by him.

John Milton "Mickey" Rivers

STORY 1- I COULD actually write another entire book just on Mickey Rivers if I had wanted to. His story is a shining example of the American Dream. He was raised by a single parent and grandmother in the Liberty City section of Miami. This is the story of how he came to be at Miami Dade.

While I was Athletics Director at Miami Dade, I interviewed and hired Joe Lee Smith for the position of Head Track Coach. Joe Lee Smith happened to be African-American. After I hired him and he was leaving my office, I said to him in jest, "Now that I have offered you a position, how about getting me a good black baseball player?"

Joe Lee replied seriously that he would. Two weeks later, Joe Lee called me and told me that he talked to the coach at Northwestern High and that he had a good baseball player named John Rivers. John hadn't played much baseball but had been a football player and he was a good athlete. I sent the coach at Northwestern High a questionnaire and invited John Rivers out for a visit and work-out (try-outs are legal on the junior college level).

The day arrived for John Rivers's tryout and I was heading out to the field when Birdie Tebbitts, a new area scout for the New York Mets, came to my office for a visit. I told him what I was doing and Birdie said he would come along to watch. Tony Simone, my assistant coach, threw batting practice to Rivers. John smoked line drives all over the field. Birdie and I looked at each other in amazement. This kid, with very little baseball experience, might turn out to be a real find.

After the workout, we went up to my office and I offered him a scholarship right away. I gave him an application to fill out, and I could see that he was struggling with it so I told him I would fill it out for him. I had all his information on a card he had previously given to me. I filled out the application and marked an "X" where he was to sign. Apparently John must have misunderstood or was kidding me because he marked an "X" next to it on the signature line!

Story 2- In 1968, we were on a bus trip to Panama City to play Gulf Coast Community College. Since we were traveling over our Easter break I took my wife and five children along. During a pit stop in Tallahassee at the Trailways Garage, my ten year old son Jimmy came out of the garage to tell me a man in there would not allow Johnny Rivers and David "Bro" Wilson use of the toilet facilities. I immediately went inside to see what was happening.

There was a man holding a wrench over his head screaming "that no n----- was going use these facilities." I asked the man to please allow these young men use them, but of course he would not relent. The players were very upset with this very ugly situation. The 1968 team was very close and made up of many different ethnic and racial individuals. I had no choice but to take a firm stance with this man. I told him that I would give him one minute to back off or we would physically open the area so these players could use the facilities. He refused to drop the wrench and move. Eddie Avila and Jim Didieo removed the irate man. I told John and Bro to use the facilities. Rivers took an inordinate amount of time to urinate, especially in view of the tense situation. When we got on the bus I asked Johnny, "What took you so long in there?"

He answered, "Coach, I was so nervous I couldn't go."

His remark was funny to all the guys on the team, but it was truly sad that such an incident like that could happen in the state capital of Florida. I wrote a letter to the Governor of Florida about the incident but never received a reply. I also wrote to the president of Trailways about the incident and received a very nice letter of apology, saying he would take appropriate action against the individuals involved.

Story 3- One day, in the middle of a game, the home plate umpire called me out of the dugout to tell me I needed a centerfielder. Rivers wasn't in centerfield. I asked our trainer if he knew where Rivers was. Apparently, Mickey ran out to centerfield in between innings, jumped the fence and left. I questioned one of my players, one of Mickey's close friends, and he mentioned that Rivers, along with some other students egged the Miami Dade Homecoming Queen at the recent parade. A couple of the queen's friends came to the ball park looking for Rivers. Apparently, Johnny didn't feel they were coming to only talk so he decided to leave.

Story 4- At another game, Steve Bomse, a pitcher on our club, asked to me to check Rivers's glove. Steve said Rivers was using a glove for right handed players. This seemed strange since we had already played several games and I never noticed. It was particularly alarming since he was running down all fly balls in sight and he had not made an error!

When he came into the dugout, I got his glove. Sure enough it was for a righty and Johnny was left handed. He said that he didn't have a glove and found this one on a trash pile. I had our equipment manager give Rivers a Wilson XL 2000 glove. Johnny used the glove in our next game and dropped the first ball hit to him! When he came into the dugout he threw the glove down and asked for his old glove back. Of course, we couldn't comply with his request.

Story 5- Rivers had been arrested for driving a couple of friends around in a car. What he didn't know was that his two friends had previously stolen the car. I was asked by a court appointed attorney to attend his pre-trial hearing before Judge Smith. The attorney briefed me on some questions they might ask about John. I would be under oath if and when the judge called me to testify on Johnny's behalf.

Before testifying, Judge Smith said he respected me and that what I said about Mr. Rivers would determine what he decided to do with the case. I gave some preliminary comments about Johnny. I indicated that he was basically a good person and was essentially a product of his very difficult environment. I mentioned that this young man had the potential to possibly play major league baseball. I couldn't guarantee that it would happen but he would, at least, have a chance to make something of his life. To send him to prison with hardened criminals would have been counter-productive to any chance Mickey had at a productive life.

Judge Smith thanked me for my comments. He had one question for me and it was: "Is Mr. Rivers making progress toward a degree?"

I started to run my fingers through my hair, knowing I was under oath. My answer was to be- Mr. Rivers, with hard work, is making progress toward his Associate Degree in Recreational Leadership, but I never got it all out. I said, "Judge, Mr. Rivers is making progress—"

Judge Smith interrupted me and said, "That is all want to hear."

I can't remember the legal term used but Judge Smith suspended the sentence for John Rivers, with no record of a felony conviction. Judge Smith told me I would be somewhat a surrogate guardian of Mr. Rivers and would be accountable for his actions. Needless to say, I had a long conversation with John about his future behavior. Rivers went on to play 15 years in the Major Leagues of course, and in 1978, when the Yankees played the Dodgers in the World Series, Judge Smith contacted Mickey requesting a signed baseball for his Grandson! That year, the Miami Herald wrote a very emotional human interest story about Mickey Rivers and how he overcame adversity to become a very productive citizen. I was mentioned as having a hand in his development. Later, I received an anonymous letter saying that my motivation for helping Mickey Rivers was for my own selfish reasons and that winning baseball games was my real motivation. Needless to say, that was the last anonymous letter that I ever read. Remember, you're never going to please everybody.

Story 6- Mickey was blessed with a great deal of natural ability. His instincts were cat-like. When hitting, Mickey would over stride very badly with his leg even though he always kept his hands back. I received a very important lesson in over coaching when I tried to lessen his leg stride. All it did was to take his hitting aggressiveness away from him. After a month of completely confusing him, I told him to forget all I told him about over striding with his leg. I pointed to the field and told him just to go out and relax and play baseball.

Years later Tommy Lasorda attended a clinic at the American Baseball Coaches Convention where the speaker was talking in glowing and highly technical terms about the ways in which you can teach agility. Tommy leaned over to me and said, "I could just see you trying to coach Mickey Rivers when you had him with these drills". Tommy's comments only reinforced my thinking about over coaching. I could have ruined Rivers future Major League career before it got started had I allowed my ego get in the way of good common sense. Agility drills may help some athletes to sharpen their skills, but the innate ability has to be there to develop.

Story 7- Mickey was signed by the Atlanta Braves for $3000 in 1969, but he was eventually traded to the Angels. Red Smith, the Angel's Scout came to my office one day to inquire where he could contact Rivers. I sent David "Bro" Wilson with Red Smith over to John's house. Red informed me that the General Manager of the Angels wanted him to fly Rivers out to Phoenix for the Instructional League. After the Instructional League was over, Rivers was going to be put up in a motel in Anaheim, paid a stipend and at his leisure keep in shape. The club felt that having him in Anaheim would help them to keep an eye on his activities.

The next day Red came to my office again looking for Rivers, and I was surprised to hear that he was not already on his way to Phoenix. Red said that he and John had a lay over in Houston airport before getting the connecting flight to Arizona. Rivers told Red that he had to go to the Men's room and that he would be right back. When the flight to Phoenix was to board, John Rivers was a no show. I called Rivers immediately.

His answer as to why he didn't board the plane was "that he was already home sick for his family and friends."

I told him he was going to blow a good opportunity to further his professional career. I made him come to my office as soon as possible so he could go to Arizona with Red.

Story 8- After Johnny's first complete year in the Major Leagues, he came to my office for a visit. I was happy to see that in his last game against the Tigers he had four or five hits off Mickey Lolich. I asked him how he liked hitting off such a tough left handed pitcher. The way he answered me, I got the impression he didn't even know how formidable a pitcher Lolich was. I got the impression from this and other conversations we had down the road that he was unaware of the magnitude of success he was having in the Major Leagues. In his own mind, he thought he was playing in some industrial league! I am convinced that this low key approach was a factor in his success.

Story 9 - I had a phone call from Bro Wilson who told me he saw Mickey at a city park playing tackle football wearing nothing but a t-shirt! I called Mickey to verify what Bro had told me. He said he was only playing some fun football with his buddies. I told him that such foolish behavior could lead to a serious injury and that could end his big league career, so he took my advice and stopped playing tackle football.

Story 10 – The coaches and players and Miami Dade used to call him the "weather man" because he liked to imitate one of the local television meteorologists. Later, my son John was in Detroit with his University of New Orleans team that he played on. They were to play there in the NCAA tournament. John and a group of New Orleans players decided to go to the Yankees-Tigers. Mickey was in the on deck circle ready to lead off when John, in a field box close to the field, tried to get Rivers attention by yelling "Mickey! Mickey!" Rivers did not respond until he yelled "Weather Man!" Rivers came over to the box and was talking with John until the umpire had to yell over to him to get into the box so they could start the game! That was vintage Rivers – an umpire interrupting a conversation with a friend in order to start a big league game!

Story 11- I attended the 1977 World Series in Cincinnati because Mickey Rivers was playing for the Yankees at the time. The night before the opening game, I was attending a social gathering, where I sat at a table with Tommy Lasorda and Dick Young, the famous sports writer of the New York Daily News. I believe he later became a writer with the New York Times.

Tommy introduced me to Dick as Mickey Rivers's college coach. Dick commenced to tell me that Mickey wasn't one of his favorite players because he was stuck on himself and it was hard to get any information out of him. I respectfully disagreed with Dick's opinion. Mickey was a very shy person and didn't feel comfortable talking to media people and individuals he didn't know well. I made a genuine effort to convince him that Mickey was a great guy and was, by no means, stuck on himself. In fact, Dick's analysis of Mickey was the opposite of the way he really was. Mickey was a very gregarious person when with friends. He was also very congenial to fans and youngsters wanting his autograph or pictures with him. I personally witnessed his sincere kindness to adult fans and youngsters seeking the above.

From Left to Right: Bucky Dent, Me, Mickey Rivers, and Joe Garagiola-Photo: Courtesy of New York Yankees' Media Dept.

Russell "Bucky" Dent

Story 1- Bucky was a pretty good running back at Hialeah High School. In fact, he played very little baseball because of spring football practice. Spring football practice on the high school level is allowed in the state of Florida. It was not until Bucky's senior year that his baseball prowess was being recognized. I was a real good friend of Martin Frady his baseball coach at Hialeah. Marty had sent me some pretty good players over the years. In talking to Coach Frady, he mentioned that Bucky had already signed a Letter of Intent to play football at the University of Tennessee at Martin. Since Bucky was not living at home but rather with the Don Roper family in Hialeah, I was a little reluctant to recruit Bucky. I frankly thought it would be in his best interest to go away to college in order to play football.

One day, however, I had a phone call from Coach Frady in which he indicated that Bucky was leaning towards playing college baseball. I arranged to meet Bucky the next day in Coach Frady's office. I mentioned to Bucky that I could understand his being confused about going the football or the baseball route. I asked him, "Do you feel that you could be a running back someday in the National Football League?"

His answered, "I don't think that I am big or fast enough to do so."

I told him if he were to go the baseball route, he would, at least, have a chance to play in the Major Leagues. On the other hand, because of his size and lack of foot speed, the National Football League was not a possibility. At the end of our conversation, Bucky verbally committed to play baseball at Miami Dade. Unbelievably after that, Jim Powell, Head Football at Hialeah High School and a good friend of mine, would not allow Bucky to continue to use the weight room at the high school because he changed his mind about playing college football!

Story 2- Before Bucky matriculated at Miami Dade, he was drafted by the Saint Louis Cardinals but declined their offer. While in school, Bucky made himself into a better baseball player. He would take one hundred grounders a day. He was the only player on my club that loved to hit off Steve Carlton when he threw to hitters in game like situations. Carlton, who worked out with our club before going to spring training, was a real challenge to hit during those sessions, but Bucky always hung tough against him.

Story 3- After one season at Miami Dade, Bucky was signed by Walt Widmayer. Bucky was the first of a long line of my players to be signed by the Chicago White Sox. In fact, so many were signed by Walt Widmayer that the media referred to Miami Dade as being a farm club of the White Sox. Due to this close relationship, Roland Hemond, General Manager of the White Sox, made it possible for Miami Dade to play their major league club each year when they came to play the Baltimore Orioles in Miami during spring training. We always played them tough. One year we lost 5-4 to them in a great night game on our campus. It was a tremendous experience for our players to play before a big crowd. My son Paul, who was playing for us, had two hits. Bucky was playing before many of his friends from Hialeah. The Miami Herald covered the game with a big story. In the story the reporter covering the game asked Bucky what it was like playing for Coach Mainieri. He said it was a great experience but that I was a tough disciplinarian and that I was very competitive and hated to loose. He said that "Coach Mainieri would not talk to me for two weeks after I struck out with the bases loaded in the Florida State Junior College Tournament."

When Bob Rubin, who wrote the article, mentioned the comments Bucky made about me, I answered, "Yes, Bob it is true that I didn't talk to him for two weeks but Bucky failed to tell you that he didn't come around to see me for two weeks after the incident!"

Bucky and I went fishing a few times when he played for me. I was like a surrogate father to Bucky during a very formative time in his career. Needless to say, Bucky Dent and I have remained close friends to this day.

Story 4- In 1978, I saw Mickey Rivers and Bucky Dent play in the World Series in New York. I was having breakfast with Bucky at his home in Wyckoff, New Jersey the day before the third game. I asked him if he was nervous playing in his first World Series.

He said "Heck no, playing in the World Series is a piece of cake after playing for you. You prepared me well on how to handle pressure! In fact, I sometimes wonder if I would ever have had the opportunity to play in the Major Leagues if I had not played for a guy like you. So many people in Hialeah tried to dissuade me from going to play for you because of your reputation as a hard nosed coach. I thank God that I never listened to them because, I would probably not be here today talking about playing the World Series."

Story 5- Bucky asked me to talk to Mickey before the third game of the 1978 World Series because Mickey said he was hurt and wasn't going to play the rest of the Series. Apparently, he was upset because George Steinbrenner thought he played poorly in the first two Series loses in Los Angeles. I couldn't believe that he needed a talk from me to help him so many years after he played for me in college. At any rate, I talked to him and indicated that sitting out was not an option. He would be letting his fellow teammates down and he should be strong enough to forget about what George Steinbrenner said, or was suppose to have said or did, and just play baseball. Both Mickey and Bucky ended up playing noteworthy roles in the New York Yankees winning the 1978 World Series against Tommy Lasorda's Dodgers.

Bob Stinson

Story 1- Bob was a high profile prospect coming out of Miami High School but decided to enhance his chances of getting a better signing bonus by attending Miami Dade. He came to me as a very talented centerfielder. We annually finished our fall work-outs by playing an all star team of Cuban major league players living in the Miami area. The game was played at a City of Miami baseball park. Players such as Orlando Pena, Tony Gonzalez, Bert Campinaros, Carlos Pascual and others played in the game.

Since there was no major league free agent draft in 1965, there were twenty-five major league scouts in attendance. It was a good opportunity for the scouts to see our prospects play against top level competition. Bob played centerfield for our club, and in the third inning a hard grounder was hit to center that went through his legs. Bob ***trotted*** after the ball. When he came into the dugout, I told him that, since he was so tired that he couldn't run full speed after the ball, he could just trot on home. My coaching philosophy was to never get on my players for physical errors but I felt that lack of hustle and playing hard could not be tolerated. I am certain that I infuriated many of the scouts in attendance for taking this action. I explained to Bob why I was so adamant in my disciplining him and told him that some day he would be thankful that I treated him in that manner.

Three years later, when he was in professional baseball playing in the Pacific Coast League, I received a very nice letter from Bobby thanking me for what I did. He mentioned that he remembered me every day when he went out the tunnel to the field to play. My disciplinary action in 1965 convinced him never to walk or trot on a baseball field again. When I saw him play in the major leagues over his twelve-plus year career, he always sprinted to and from his position. My stand on hustle was tough to take sometimes, but I always told my players that when I got on them to play hard, I would do it because I wanted them to be a better player and person. This is what I call "tough love!"

Story 2- We started our regular season in the spring of 1966 playing very poorly. I had recruited three catchers and I rotated all three in our early games. One catcher could throw but couldn't hit, one couldn't catch or hit, and one couldn't catch, throw or hit. I was at wits end.

The day before our next game, I lined up three complete sets of catching gear. I then told the three catchers that I wanted to see who really wanted to catch our next game by informing them that the catcher who puts on the equipment the fastest, would catch the next day. They players must have thought that I had gone crazy! The ridiculous competition ended in a tie!

The next day, after conferring with Bob Stinson, he became our starting catcher. This conversion was instrumental in our team going to the Junior College World Series in Grand Junction, Colorado. We finished second in Grand Junction after losing a heart breaking final game. This story in itself will be told later in the chapter.

Kurt Bevacqua

Story 1- A book could be written entirely on this player's noteworthy career. Kurt was probably the best clutch hitter I ever coached. His lack of defensive skills probably kept him from being a regular player in the big leagues, but he did spend fourteen years as a utility player, which is quite an achievement.

One day we were tied in the thirteenth inning in a game against Broward Community College. I was pacing up and down the dugout when Kurt said to me, "Doc, sit down and relax because I am going to end this game with a home run." His next time at bat, he hit a towering home run that must have traveled five hundred feet!

Story 2- We were playing Manatee Community College at the Junior College Tournament in Panama City in 1967 and we were losing 2-1 in the last inning. We had one runner on while Coach Bob Wynn of Manatee was out at the mound ready to make a pitching change. In their bull pen warming up was the hard throwing ace of the staff and a soft throwing right handed pitcher that was known to have control problems. Kurt was on deck and he screamed, "Coach bring your ace, we want your ace!"

I said, "Kurt keep your mouth shut. We want the soft throwing guy that can't throw strikes."

Apparently, Coach Wynn heard him and brought in his ace. Kurt hit a two run walk off home run to win the game. That was vintage Kurt. He was very cocky, but he usually backed his behavior with his clutch hitting. Such clutch hitting by Kurt Bevacqua beat Manatee in the 1966 when he had two home runs in the Florida Junior College Tournament. He had a penchant for hitting home runs in clusters, just like he did when he hit a couple of home runs while playing for the San Diego Padres in the World Series against the Detroit Tigers in the 1984.

Story 3 – In the summer of 1969, while Kurt was playing professionally in the minor leagues, my phone rang at two in the morning. When I answered the phone it was Kurt Bevacqua and his comment was, "Doc, I just had two home runs tonight and a third missed by three feet in a game in Savannah, Georgia."

I said, "Great Kurt but why couldn't you wait to call me at a more respectable time. We've been very tired because my father-in-law had a heart attack recently and we've been on edge."

He said, "Doc, you are like a father to me, and I wanted to share this with you- aren't you happy for me?"

I replied, "Yes Kurt, I am always happy to hear about your accomplishments but please call at a more respectable time in the future."

There is no question that I was a surrogate father figure to Kurt Bevacqua during this phase of his life.

Story 4 – One day we were playing when we had gale like winds on campus. An opposing player hit a gigantic home over our one hundred foot Australian pine trees in right field. I heard someone yelling, "I got it, I got it!" I checked with one of my assistants and he said, "You heard correctly. It was Bevacqua yelling, I got it, I got it".

When Kurt came into the dugout, I asked him "Why were you yelling, I got it, I got it, when the ball went over the trees?"

His answer was, "The ball started over me before it got caught up in the wind and went over the trees."

I said, "How could the ball carry that far from where you were playing?"

He kept insisting that he was serious, and I said he had "a bird brain".

After the game, he asked to talk to me. With tears in his eyes he said "Your remark hurt me because you are such a father figure to me and I look up to you so much."

I told him I was sorry I hurt his feelings and hoped he would accept my heart felt and sincere apology. I never again made such a stupid remark during the remainder of my coaching career. Fortunately, to this day Kurt and I remain very close and I visit him in San Diego every chance I get.

Story 5 – I came to find out from players who played with Kurt in professional baseball that he was still a fun loving guy who could play a joke with the best of them. Willie Stargell, Manny Sanguillen, and Kurt of the Pirates were playing winter ball in the Caribbean one year. They were dressed in their uniforms in front of the hotel where they were staying waiting for a taxi to take them to the ball park. Across the street from the hotel was a trailer truck with coffins loaded on it. Kurt pulled Willie off to the side and told him to bet Manny $500 that dead people were in those coffins loaded on that truck across the street. He told Willie that he would get in the last coffin on the right and that after Manny takes the bet, bring him down to the coffin in question to prove there were real dead people in those coffins. Manny took the bet and Stargell took him to the coffin where Bevacqua was lying on his back. Willie opened the coffin for Manny to see and when he did, blurted out "Boo"! According to Willie, Sanguillen almost jumped out of his uniform!

Story 6- Kurt told me that he had a big beautiful house in the San Diego area while he was playing for the Padres. This house had two big double entrance doors leading into his living room. One Christmas, he gave his wife, Carrie, a nice Mercedes car and drove it through the front door and put it next to the Christmas tree! Kurt hasn't changed over the years!

Randy Bush

Story 1- My plan was to recruit Bush from Carol City High School and another kid named Randy Johnson from Hialeah High School. Both made the Miami Dade All County Team in the local papers. Both came to my office so I could discuss their scholarship opportunities. I talked to Johnson first. I mentioned that I was going to recruit both he and Randy Bush. I told him that I would play both of them at first base and at the end of fall work-outs, I would determine who the better first baseman was and the other person, if he hit well, would play in the outfield. I asked him how he viewed my plan. He responded that the baseball coach of the Miami Dade- South Campus said he could play first base there. I said it appeared that he was bent on going to Miami Dade-South campus in light of this disclosure. I shook his hand and wished him good luck. I mentioned, in a kidding fashion, I hoped that we would could remain friends and that we could wave to each when he traveled south on the Palmetto Expressway as I passed him traveling north to Miami Dade North.

After I finished talking to Johnson, I called Randy Bush in and started giving Bush the same scenario, but did not inform him how my conversation ended with Johnson. Half way through my discussing the plan with Randy Bush, he indicated, with out hesitation, that he welcomed the pending competition. He mentioned that he had always wanted to play for me since he had followed my team since he was a youngster. Randy Bush had a very productive career as a first baseman at Miami Dade North, and after his experience with me, he played at the University of New Orleans. He signed with the Minnesota Twins and played ten years in the Major Leagues. The Twins, during Bush's tenure with them, won two world championships. Randy Johnson had a very good career as an outfielder at Miami Dade South. In addition, he had a "cup of coffee" in the Major Leagues.

Story 2- After Randy completed his career with me he wasn't drafted by a professional club. I was discouraged, but probably not nearly as much as Randy was. Randy Bush not being drafted was particularly disturbing for me because he had two great years at Miami Dade North. Even with all the contacts I had with professional scouts, I couldn't get anyone to draft him. In fact, I remember a conversation that I had with Walt Widmayer of the White Sox. Somehow Randy Johnson's name came up and Walt said Johnson was a better prospect than Randy Bush. I bet him a steak dinner that Bush would be more successful in professional baseball than Johnson, although at that time I had no idea how we were going to get Bush into pro ball. Years later, after both careers unfolded, Walt was very gracious in paying our bet. The steak, at a very classy restaurant in Lakeland, Florida, was well appreciated.

Since Bush wasn't drafted, I wanted him to go to a senior college in a different professional scouting area, because scouts in another region might feel differently about him. Randy accepted a scholarship offer from Coach Ron Maestri at the University of New Orleans.

During the summer of 1978, Randy played for me at Wareham in the Cape Cod League. He got off to poor start. I had a long talk with him and found that he was still brooding from the draft. He was feeling sorry for himself so I got on him and said to start playing up to his capabilities while in the Cape and then go on to New Orleans like we planned. By the end of the summer he was selected as the best prospect in Cape Cod League. He went on to New Orleans, and after a great career, signed for a nice bonus with the Twins. Randy met and married Cathy who was from New Orleans. The rest is history!

Randy Bush- Photo: Courtesy of Twins Media Dept.

Ray Bare

Story 1- I recruited Ray out of Miami Southwest High School. He was a very intelligent individual with outstanding potential as a pitcher. He turned out to be one of the hardest throwers I ever coached. His fastball was absolutely explosive! He was drafted out of high school so there was a great deal of interest by the area scouts while he was with me. In his first year (1968), he didn't get to pitch much early in the season because he had shoulder problems. The scouts continually phoned me wanting to know when he was going to pitch. Once his shoulder came around, I brought him around slowly and finally gave him a start at Edison Community College, under the lights, in Fort Myers. He was outstanding that night, striking out twenty batters. You could actually hear his fast ball humming!

Something funny happened in the last of the ninth inning. A pinch hitter was sent up to hit and Ray uncorked one of his ninety-five miles per hour fast balls, but the umpire called it a ball. The Edison Community College hitter turned around to the umpire and said, "Mr. Umpire that was a strike. Call it up; I want to get out of here alive!" Everyone in the ball park could hear it and started to laugh.

Story 2- During the Fall of 1968, Ray continued to have sporadic arm problems. We sent him to see a couple of different orthopedic surgeons who could not find what was wrong with his shoulder. They must not have had MRI machines in 1967. At the conclusion of our fall work-outs, the coaching staff met with Ray Bare relative to his future in our program. The doctors had indicated to me that they could not determine the cause of his arm problems and since he could not pitch without pain, he might want to consider giving up baseball and spend more quality time on his studies. Ray was adamant that he wanted to continue his collegiate career even if he had to work through the pain. That was fine with me. It was a challenge that I was prepared to face with Ray.

In 1969, Ray had a great season. We played Manatee Community College in the finals of the Florida Junior College Tournament. The games were played on our campus. In one of the games, Ray was locked in a pitchers duel with Pat Osborne. Both Osborne and Ray, after their collegiate careers, played in the Major Leagues. In fact, a total of seven players on that field that day eventually played in the big leagues. Miami Dade had three (Ray Bare with the Cardinals and Tigers; Mickey Rivers with the Angels, Yankees, and Rangers; Glenn Borgmann with the Twins). Manatee had four (John Grubb; Pat Osborne; Mac Scarce; Ron Cash).

In the ninth inning of the championship game, a hard grounder was hit up the middle and Ray Bare tried to field it, but the ball took a bad bounce and ran up his arm, hitting him in the throat. He collapsed in pain. He finally got up and I put my arm around Ray, telling him that I had to take him out of the game. His answer to me was, "No coach, I'm staying in the game because I want to prove that I can pitch with a little pain."

The trainer cleared him and Ray finished the inning, after which we had a heavy rain storm. I mentioned this game earlier, if you will remember. The game was delayed for three days. We finally lost to Manatee 2-1 in 15 innings! Since Ray was a hard thrower, I was not able to bring him back with three days rest, because I was afraid that small amount of rest could damage his arm even further. On the other hand, Pat Osborne, a crafty, soft throwing left hander, was able to come back and beat us. Ray went on to be a major leaguer. I feel that his determination to continue to pitch after being hit in the throat that game was related to the conversation we had in my office the fall before. Years later, he told me that conversation was a very defining moment in his career.

Story 3 – Ray and I stayed in touch over the years and one day he mentioned that he wanted to get back into baseball in some capacity. I was now retired from Miami Dade and was working as a scout for the Milwaukee Brewers and told him that I would make some phone calls on his behalf.

I was doing free agent scouting in South Florida and covering the Pacific Coast League from my second home in Colorado Springs. My son, Paul, had become the head baseball coach at the Air Force Academy in Colorado so it was a good arrangement for me professionally and for the family. One day, I had a very shocking phone call from Charlie Nobles of the Miami News. He informed me that Ray Bare was seriously ill at Baptist Hospital in Miami. He mentioned that they thought Ray was terminally ill with leukemia and his only hope was a bone marrow transplant. Ray requested that Charlie contact me because he wanted to talk to me. I flew back from Colorado the next day. Rosetta and I visited Ray as soon as we arrived in Miami. He confided in me and we talked about his condition, the prognosis, the transplant, his family and his will to live. Rosetta and I prayed with Ray for strength and tried our best to help him during this very trying time in his life. He mentioned that Sparky Anderson, his manager with the Tigers, called periodically. We talked about old times. He asked me to contact Mickey Rivers who was his teammate at Miami Dade. He wanted Mickey to come visit him. I contacted Mickey regarding my conversation with Ray. Mickey did get to visit Ray before he died. My wife and I visited Ray in the hospital four times. In our last visit with him, he told us a donor could not be found. His sister had been his only hope, and unfortunately, they found she was not a complete match. Raymond Bare passed away, peacefully, at the age of forty-one. He left a wife and two children. In my mind, with all his suffering and courage, he left this life on earth a real winner and an inspiration to all who knew and loved him.

Mike Piazza

Mike initially enrolled at the University of Miami, and as a freshman had only fourteen at bats. Tommy Lasorda called on the phone and asked if I was interested in Mike, who wanted to transfer. I was a little upset with Tommy because Mike didn't come with me out of high school and I asked why Mike had not come with me initially. Tommy mentioned that Mike's mother wanted him to go to a four year college. I understood Mrs. Piazza's feelings, and told Tommy that Mike should inform Coach Fraser of his intentions before calling me. Mike Piazza transferred to Miami Dade and had a banner year with us. He played first base and hit with power even after hurting his hand on a tag play at first base.

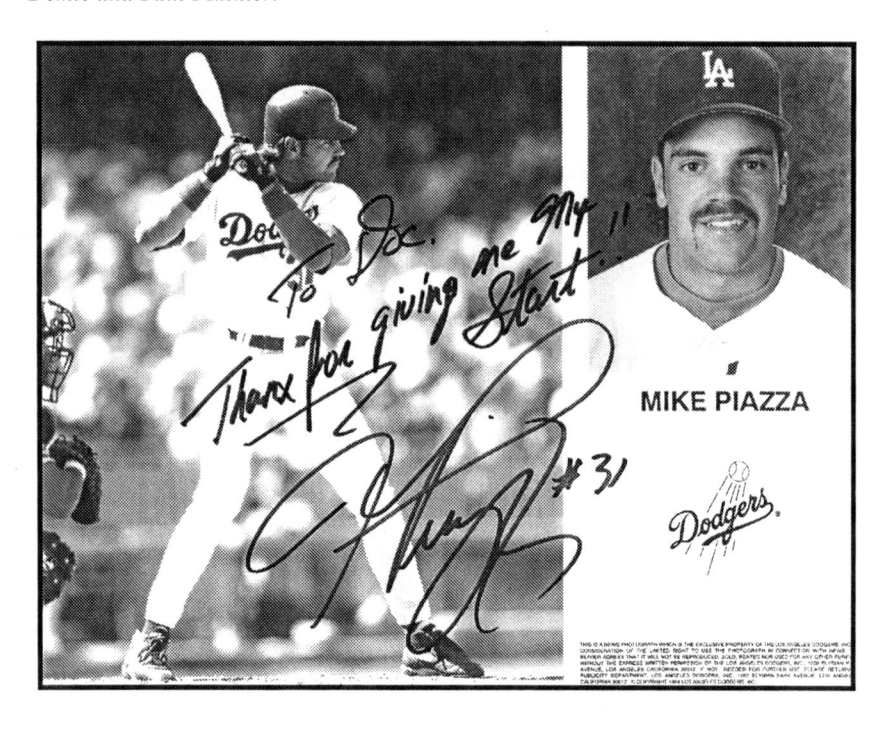

Photos: Courtesy of Los Angeles Dodgers & Bob Bailey of Miami Dade

Mike had great arm strength and I thought he should convert to catcher. He agreed with my recommendation. In talking with Mike and my son Paul, who was coaching at Saint Thomas, it was agreed that Mike would transfer to Saint Thomas and catch, but this was a contingency plan in case Mike did not get drafted.

Mike ended up being drafted in the sixty-first round by the Dodgers. He flew out to Los Angeles and worked out at Dodger Stadium under watchful eyes of Dodger bigwigs Tommy Lasorda, Joe Blaney and Ben Wade. Mike put on a good display of power and handled himself well around first base, but Blaney and Wade thought he was at best, a journeyman type first baseman. Tommy asked them if they would consider him a prospect if he was a shortstop, but they thought he was too big and too slow footed. Tommy then asked them if they would like him as a prospect if he was a catcher, and they said it was a possibility.

Mike Piazza signed for a modest bonus and went off to play professional baseball. He spent a period of time at the Dodger's

Baseball Academy in the Dominican Republic learning how to catch under Mike Scioscia. This was quite an accomplishment considering that he had to live in a dormitory with seventy-five Latin players that spoke no English! The rest is history. Mike Piazza will go down as one of the most prolific hitting catchers to ever play the game and will enter the Hall of Fame once eligible. In fact, he broke the home run record for catchers during the 2004 season while playing for the New York Mets. The Mets had a night, June 18, 2004, at Shea Stadium honoring Mike for breaking the record. They invited all the living Hall of Fame catchers e.g. Gary Carter; Johnny Bench; Carlton Fisk; Yogi Berra; Ivan Rodriguez; and Lance Parrish. I was honored when Mike insisted that my wife and I be invited by the Mets to the event. The Hall of Famers, Mike, the Mets' Manager, General Manager, Owner, Tommy Lasorda, and I were all on the field. We were introduced to the sell out crowd prior to the New York Mets - Detroit Tigers game. I was introduced as Mike's college coach. I was overjoyed to be part of such a first class event. This was a great evening for Mike. He is to be commended for his achievements because he worked hard to reach this pinnacle of success.

From Left to Right: Me, Mike Piazza, and Art Howe- Photos: Courtesy of Jay Horwitz, VP Media Relations, New York Mets

Left to Right: Gary Carter, Johnny Bench, Carlton Fisk, Mike Piazza, Yogi Berra, Pudge Rodriguez, and Lance Parrish- Photo Courtesy of NY Mets Media

As I sat on that field waiting for Mike to be justly honored, I couldn't help but remember the conversation I had with Mike when I coached him in college. Mike had hit some unbelievable solo home runs in games early in that season when we were winning games by a large margin. I thought he needed to hit more consistently in clutch situations. He needed to be challenged more, and I asked him point blank, "Mike when are you going to hit some of those home runs when they really mean something?" All these home runs are great, but they don't mean anything unless they are coming in clutch situations."

He replied with a firm and determined voice, "Doc, I'll prove to you that I can hit in the clutch."

He made me a believer then, and he has proved that he is a clutch hitter during his major league career. I pray to God that I'll be in Cooperstown when he is inducted into the Hall of Fame!

Dennis Hegarty

This player was a walk-on from New Jersey during our 1966 season. During our fall workouts, Dennis Hegarty showed no natural tools to play college baseball. At the end of fall, I tried to discourage him from continuing his quest to be a member of our team. Dennis would not quit so I allowed him to continue to workout with our club. Well into the spring, he was still with us working toward earning a uniform. Every day he was at practice working out in this gray sweat suit he had. One day I finally told one of my assistants, Tony Simone, to give Hegarty a uniform. Frankly, I was sick and tired seeing this player in his baggy sweat pants.

Dennis played sparingly for us in 1966, until our regular leftfielder had a serious injury in the Florida State Junior College Tournament. I don't know what it was other than pure determination, but Dennis played well in the Junior College World Series in Grand Junction, Colorado. In fact, he hit a home run against Phoenix College in the thirteenth inning to beat them 2-1! The home run was off Gary Gentry, who later pitched for the New York Mets.

In 1967, the player Hegarty had replaced came back and had every right to inherit his job in leftfield. He name was Preston Pratt and he was a very talented player with questionable desire. He ran well and hit for power as a switch hitter. After stretching my patience with his indifference and after many warnings, I dismissed him from the team. The next morning a couple leaders from our team, Terry Brumfield and Joe Arnold, came to my office with Dennis Hegarty and pleaded for Preston to be given another chance. They felt that he could help our club, but more importantly, we could be helping Pratt to grow up. I asked Hegarty if he was aware that by Preston coming back, he could lose his spot in left field. Dennis said he realized that, but he felt that in the best interest of the club and Preston Pratt, we should allow him to return.

Dennis Hegarty received a scholarship to Ohio University and was instrumental in taking them to the College World Series. He later became Head Baseball Coach at Plymouth High School in Ohio. Preston Pratt played at Southern Illinois University. He never fulfilled his baseball potential but did become a very successful pilot.

Unselfish individuals, like Dennis Hegarty, make coaching a rewarding profession.

Nick Belmonte

This player didn't have a fluid swing and was an average defensive leftfielder, but he could run and had first step quickness. I was loaded with outfielders in 1973. In my conference with him after fall workout, I tried to encourage him to pursue activities other than baseball. I tried to convince him that his chances of playing much baseball in the spring were very slim. Of course, Nick would not buy into my evaluation. He pleaded with me to give him another shot in the spring. Somehow, I always had a soft spot in my heart for players who were willing to persevere under such insurmountable odds.

He forced his way into our lineup by taking advantage of the few opportunities given him, and he became our regular leftfielder in 1973. He was instrumental in leading our team to a runner-up spot in the 1974 Junior College World Series. He later played at the University of Florida on a scholarship. He holds the single season stolen base record in the Southeastern Conference. He is now a college color baseball commentator for a couple of television stations. In addition, he is the Personnel Director for The Independent Northern Baseball League. He also puts on baseball base running clinics throughout the United States. Young aspiring baseball players should use former players like Nick Belmonte as role models.

Tim Hulett

I saw Hulett play, as a member of the University of South Florida baseball team, against my son Paul's University of New Orleans team. He was a really talented player that had professional potential. The father of one of Paul's teammates, John Shiave, was sitting in the stands next to me, and he started to discuss Tim Hulett. He knew all about Hulett since they both came from Springfield, Illinois. Both of us felt that Tim's professional baseball potential may not be adequately developed at the University of South Florida. A couple of weeks later, I had a call from John Shiave and he indicated that he talked to Hulett's father and his son was thinking about transferring. He wanted to know if I was interested in Tim transferring to Miami Dade. I said that I would be interested only if his Coach Robin Roberts agreed to release him. A couple of days later, I had a call from Robin Roberts and he thought Timmy could better prepare for a professional baseball career by playing for me. Robin was very cordial to me and had a genuine interest in wanting to help Tim Hulett. In fact, Robin showed his sincerity and interest in Hulett's career by phoning me several times to ask how Timmy was doing. I found out later that Robin originally came from Springfield, Illinois, and knew the Hulett family well. Robin Roberts, a member of the Hall of Fame, is one of the classiest people that I have met in baseball. Tim Hulett had a very productive career in the major leagues while playing with the White Sox and Orioles. He achieved success because of natural talent and a tremendous work ethic.

Left to Right: Joel McKeon, John Cangelosi, and Tim Hulett
Photo: Courtesy of Chicago White Sox

Dave McCammon

This player had as much major league potential as any of my former players that made it to the big leagues, but his poor attitude prevented him from making it to the major leagues. Dave had a tremendous Junior College World Series in 1964. He hit two or three home runs in that tournament. In fact, Mayo Smith, a Yankee scout, told me that McCammon had future super star major league talent.

After we won the 1964 Junior College World Series, the Houston organization flew Dave and me out to Paul Richards' home in Texas so that the club could work him out. Paul Richards was the General Manager of the Houston club. He and I sat in the first base dugout while one of his coaches, Clint Courtney, threw batting practice. McCammon put on a display of awesome power. Courtney then had Dave take some fly balls in centerfield. He looked great out there. He caught everything in sight. Paul asked me, "Where did you play this guy?"

I said, "Leftfield."

Richards said, "If you played this guy in leftfield the way he runs down fly balls, you must have had a great centerfielder and I'll sign him sight unseen."

I said, "You have a deal". Dave Magnole, our centerfielder, signed for a small bonus and played well in the Houston organization.

After the workout, Mr. Richards talked to Dave and me in his car before heading to the airport. Richards mentioned to Dave that he was prepared to make him an offer. He indicated that Eddie Robinson, his special assistant, would contact him in Miami the next week. "He will be prepared to give you $10,000 more than another clubs' best offer. We want you to be up front on the amount and Mr. Robinson will give you ten grand more than the best bonus offer (there was no free agent draft at that time). After you sign, we will send you to our rookie league team in Cocoa, Florida. The manager, Dave Philly will hit you a hundred fly balls each night after the games. If you work hard and keep your nose clean, I will move Rusty Staub to right field and start you in centerfield on opening day when we open the new Astrodome. I am telling you this in front of your college coach so there will be a clear understanding of the situation that I have lined out. This is no area scout telling you this. I am the General Manager of the club."

On the flight back to Miami, I told Dave that I hoped he understood the magnitude of Mr. Richards's offer. I hoped he would have a better attitude than the one he showed playing for me. Dave assured me that he learned a great deal about the need to have a good attitude after being at Miami Dade.

The Mainieri Factor

The following week, Mr. Robinson came to Miami and signed Dave McCammon to a lucrative contract. He reported to Cocoa, Florida to begin his profession career.

Several months later in early 1965, I had a long talk with Tony Pacheco, area scout for Houston. I asked him, "What kind of year did Dave McCammon have at Cocoa?"

He said, "Doc, you won't believe this story."

On Paul Richards's orders, Dave Philly, the manager at Cocoa, was hitting McCammon fly balls after a game. Philly had hit McCammon about seventy flies on a rather hot and humid night. The manager kept prodding Dave to keep going but he refused and said he could not continue. Apparently, the manager had other problems with Dave not responding to his coaching so he called Paul about the situation. He told Paul that McCammon was not coachable. Richards went to Cocoa to evaluate the McCammon situation and after working with him for less than an hour he left town! At the organizational meeting, Richards took McCammon off the forty man roster. This move made Dave, for all intense and purposes, a free agent. He was picked by the Dodgers and later by the Boston Red Sox. Dave McCammon, unfortunately never made the necessary adjustments to succeed in professional baseball. This is a sad case of a young person never realizing his God-given potential and not having a positive attitude.

General Manager Paul Richards and Dave McCammon- Photo: Courtesy of the Houston Media Relations Department

Harry Chappas

Story 1- This young man had more ability as a shortstop than Bucky Dent had when he played for me in college. Bucky spent over ten years in the major leagues whereas Harry spent only two and a half years in the big leagues. Harry's picture appeared on the cover of Sports Illustrated. The feature story was about how Chappas was moving along nicely in his professional career as a 5'4" shortstop. Bill Veeck, the owner of the Chicago White Sox, saw a great opportunity to market this young diminutive shortstop as a legitimate major league player. The stories that follow about Chappas give some indication why his big league career was so brief.

I recruited Harry because of his good arm, power as a switch hitter, and his outstanding speed. I tried every possible way to motivate him. I tried to encourage him in every way possible. I tried to push him hard. Nothing seemed to work. One day, he didn't charge a ground ball, and we kept him after our game to hit him several ground balls to show him how to charge it.

His biggest problem was that he wasn't punctual. I told him to invest in a good watch so he could be on time. One day, we were in Bradenton, Florida to play Manatee Community College. Several professional cross checkers flew in to see Harry play. He didn't arrive on time to board the bus so we left without him. The cross checkers at the game were livid that he wasn't there. After the game, I talked to him at the motel and asked him why he didn't make an effort to get to the ball park when he missed the bus. He had no valid excuse so he and another player who also missed the bus, did some extra running the next day. There were several incidents of insubordination during his tenure at Miami Dade. After his first and only season with me, he signed with the Chicago White Sox. He made consistent progress on the field, but Roland Hemond, the General Manager of the White Sox and Tony LaRussa, Harry's manager in AAA, said he still had difficulty with his time management.

I talked to Harry about being punctual before he was to report for spring training with the big club. I told him to get to the park three quarters of an hour before he was required to report. I passed on to Tony LaRussa the details of my talk with Harry. A couple of weeks into spring training, Rosetta and I went over to the Chicago White Sox complex to see our son play in a minor league game. We were invited out for dinner with Roland Hemond and Tony La Russa. In the course of the night, I asked how Harry Chappas was doing. Tony said, "On the first day on the field, I had all the players in the grandstand so I could explain the rules. I was talking about getting to the park on time when Harry shows up three quarters of an hour late! I was wondering if Harry was confused with your advice about getting to the park three quarters of an hour early!"

Once Harry stopped producing on the field, he was released by Chicago. I was able to get him placed with a team in Italy. I understand he broke his leg while driving a motor scooter. Apparently, his career ended at this point. A few years later, Nova High School planned to induct Harry Chappas, who graduated from Nova, into the school's Baseball Hall of Fame. I was invited by Pat McQuade, Head Baseball Coach at Nova, to present Harry at the baseball banquet. Unfortunately, Harry was a no show. I was very upset because I really liked Harry. I felt badly because I had failed to reach Harry for some reason. It was certainly a sad case of the failure of a young man, with so much promise, never being able to reach his potential.

Dave Malpeso

This player had all the tools to play in the major leagues. He was a big strong catcher with major league arm strength. He had awesome power. One game he hit a gigantic home run over the flag pole in centerfield at our home ball park which was four hundred and twenty feet from home plate! Lamar Johnson, of the Chicago White Sox, was the only other player to ever hit a home run over the centerfield fence at Mainieri Field. Dave's tools were raw but with hard work, they could have been developed. When he played at Miami Dade, the coaches had to continually remind him to do his low ball drills. In fact, I had to play him at first base because he couldn't handle our pitching staff.

His lack of a good work ethic followed him during his professional career in the Boston Red Sox organization. He continued to show some promise with the Red Sox because he was on the forty man major league roster for two years. A friend of mine, Tony Torchia, was

Dave's manager at Pawtucket, and he reiterated that Dave continued to lack a strong commitment. The General Manager of the Red Sox, Haywood Sullivan, told me that Dave's career came to an abrupt end when Manager Ralph Houk asked Dave to go up to the bullpen to catch one of the pitchers.

Malpeso responded "Skip, I can't, my hands are too tender."

That incident, I am certain, was probably the last straw and it was a sad ending to Dave Malpeso's professional career.

Dan Rohrmeier

I recruited this player as a prospective catcher. Unfortunately, he just did not have the arm or hands necessary. I played him at third base, where he did an adequate job. He was an outstanding hitter. He had power and quick hands. His loose wrists reminded you of Hank Aaron.

After playing at Miami Dade, he finished his collegiate career playing for my son, Paul, at Saint Thomas University. Due to his hitting prowess, Paul tried him at second base, but the experiment failed, and he wound up playing some outfield. He signed with the Chicago White Sox and finally had a short career in the major leagues with Seattle. While playing AAA ball in the Pacific Coast, he hit extremely well. He averaged thirty plus home runs each season while playing first base. Dan could have spent ten or more years in the major leagues had he been able to settle into a defensive position to go along with his ability at the plate. It was really a shame that he never got a legitimate chance to play regularly in the major leagues because he loved the game and played hard.

Unfortunately, he had some trouble with a manager when he was playing in the White Sox organization. This became a monkey on his back that remained for his entire professional career. It was a bad rap, even though Danny could be hard to handle at times. Once you were able to understand him, he was a pleasure to coach.

Hugo Fernandez

This young man was destined to have a very productive baseball career. He had good size, was very athletic, and was a very likeable person with a great sense of humor. Unfortunately, he never had the opportunity to fulfill this potential. At the age of nineteen, he was seriously injured, eventually losing his life, during a freak accident at our home field. During our fall workouts, we played games against other area colleges. We alternated playing the two complete teams against other colleges. The team not scheduled to play that day, took infield and batting practice on our "B" field under the supervision of one of our coaches. After they finished, they were in the process of rolling the portable batting cage into the large batting tunnel. While Coach Mansilla and the players were closing the large heavy gate, it came off the track and fell toward the players. All the players, except two, were able to run clear of the falling gate. One player, had a minor injury, but Hugo did not get completely clear of the gate. The full force of the gate hit his head. We immediately phoned for emergency assistance. Hugo was bleeding from his eyes, nose, mouth, and ears. The ambulance got to the area very quickly. Hugo was taken to North Shore Hospital. His parents arrived shortly thereafter. A neurosurgeon examined Hugo and notified the parents and me that Hugo had a very serious, life threatening head injury and that he was not expected to live. You can imagine how difficult it was for the family, the coaches, and players to accept and understand. We all prayed for a miracle but Hugo, after being on life supports for a week, passed away at the age of nineteen. My son, Paul, was the same age at the time. Losing a son or daughter, at a young age, is always difficult. It certainly puts things in perspective. There is no doubt in my mind that I was never the same coach after this tragic accident. Winning baseball games just didn't have the same importance to me. I still lined up every day as a coach and tried to prepare my teams to go out and play hard to win. I just didn't have the same passion towards winning. After Hugo's death, I still had winning teams, and many more of my former players made it to the major leagues but none of my teams ever returned to the Junior College World Series.

John Cangelosi

While I was recruiting this player, I made a visit to his home in Miami Springs. I gave him all the reasons why he should come to Miami Dade to play his baseball. He wasn't ready to play professional baseball. It was my plan to convert him into a switch hitter. In high school, he threw left handed and hit from the right side. He could better utilize his speed by hitting from the left side. In the middle of my conversation with the family, John informed me that he wanted to sign with me. His mother said, "Johnny, are you sure that you want to play for Coach Mainieri? You know you have heard from several people that he is a hard nosed coach. I don't want you to come home and complain to me about him being hard on you."

John still signed and had a very productive career. He played right field which is tough, because it the sun field. Odibbe McDowell, who later played in the major leagues, played centerfield. Many times, Johnny wanted to give up hitting left handed. I made him stay with the program. John Cangelosi played ten years in the big leagues. Not bad for a player that no scout was interested in until he became a switch hitter.

Jim Hendry

After Jim graduated from Spring Hill College in Mobile, Alabama, he took a position as an assistant in baseball and football at Columbus High School in Miami. In the spring of 1978, I was putting a staff together since I was going to coach Wareham in the Cape Cod League. At the dinner table I mentioned to my son, John, who was on the baseball team at Columbus, that I was looking for a young coach to assist me with the Wareham club the coming summer. I wanted someone that could throw batting practice because I couldn't throw any more on account of a bad shoulder.

John said, "There is a coach at Columbus, Jim Hendry that would fit the bill for you. He is a real fire ball with a lot of energy."

I asked John to check with him to see if he was interested. "If he appears to be interested, tell him that I would be happy to meet with him after his play-off game at Mark Light Stadium on Friday."

There, I introduced myself to Jim and before I could start to explain the deal to him, his comment was, "When are we leaving?"

This was a surely a clear indication to me that this guy was really going to be very energetic person to have on the staff.

Jim gave me only one request. He requested that I not give him a collateral job where he would have to climb a ladder, because he had a fear of heights. I arranged a job working for the local board of education. The first day on the job, they had Jim carry roof singles up the ladder to a roof that they were replacing. That night at our first team workout, Jim pulled me aside and said, "Doc you have to get me off the job you arranged for me before I kill myself going up and down that ladder!" Jim was visibly shaken so I immediately had him transferred to a land based job.

We spent a great summer coaching together. He really showed me his dedication to baseball by throwing batting practice every night without the benefit of a protective screen! I confess that I was not really testing his toughness and dedication with this arrangement. The owner of the club just wouldn't buy us a screen.

About three weeks into the season, my wife was hospitalized in Gloucester, which is north of Boston, with a blood clot in her lung. She was in the hospital for two weeks. The first week she was in the intensive care unit. Her condition was guarded so I had to commute to and from Boston. I turned the Wareham club over to the rookie coach, Jim Hendry, with the comment, "It is all yours Jim, don't screw it up!" Jim did a great job filling in for me. The more I worked with him, the more respect I had for him as a good baseball man and as a person.

After the season was over, Jim asked if I thought he had a future in the game. He was, at that time, contemplating taking a position in television broadcasting, since he majored in that area in college. I assured him that he had the potential to go far in the game of baseball. I said that I would hire him in a minute if I had an opening. I encouraged him to enroll in the Sports Administration masters program at Saint Thomas University in Miami.

Jim Hendry's rise up the baseball ladder was the result of innate ability, intestinal fortitude, hard work, dedication, and honesty. Now with the Cubs, Jim and Andy MacPhail were a perfect fit. Jim is a workaholic and Andy had been a great mentor for an aspiring, young general manager. Andy Mac Phail left the Cubs at the end of the 2006 season. John McDonough became Acting President of the club and Jim and John moved quickly to make the Cubs a legitimate National League contender.

Jim is fearless. He will make deals or trades with a very positive approach. As I mentioned, he is an upfront type of person. He relates extremely well with players, managers, and front office personnel. When he tells you something or promises you something, you can take it to the bank. He is a good listener but acts with conviction. He knows what it takes to win ballgames. He will make every effort to provide players that play hard and are winners for the new Cub's Manager, Lou Piniella His acquisitions of big name free agents should improve the Cubs tremendously.

He brought in Oneri Fleita, former Miami Dade and Creighton player, as Farm Director. He has and will continue to develop players that are fundamentally sound and play the game hard.

Jim has paid his dues. He made Creighton an instant winner and took them to the College World Series. He has worked at all levels of professional baseball under some top notch baseball people like Gary Hughes, Dave Dombrowski, and Andy MacPhail. Jim's success was due to all the reasons outlined above, but the turning point in his career was his ability to see the windows of opportunity before him and having the foresight to take advantage of those opportunities.

The Mainieri Factor

Celebrity Golf Tournament at Doral Country Club (From Left to Right: Rick Cerone, Me, my son Paul, and Jim Hendry). Photo: courtesy of Bob Bailey-Miami Dade Media Dept.

Oneri David Fleita

Coming out of Key West High School, Oneri was considered by professional scouts to be one of the most talented left handed pitchers in Florida. Shortly after he arrived at Miami Dade, it became apparent that he had an arm injury and would never pitch for us. He was converted to the outfield and did a great job for us. He had size and good power from the left side.

In his second year with us, he got off to an awful start with the bat. I was forced to get some offense into the lineup so I started Freddy Varela as a designated hitter. Freddy took advantage of the opportunity and really hit well. I had a talk with Fleita because I wanted him to know that I appreciated the contributions he made last year. I wanted him to keep a positive attitude because there was a possibility that we would need him down the road. The answer he gave me showed his true character. In effect he said, "You are playing the right people now. They deserve to play." He said he would keep working hard and he promised that by tournament time, he would be playing regularly in right field. He was true to his word, and through sheer determination, he got himself back into the lineup and had a great second half.

After finishing his career at Miami Dade, Oneri, who had numerous scholarship offers, decided to play for Jim Hendry at the University of Creighton. He based his decision on the fact that Coach Hendry was the first coach that showed an interest in him. This was a wise decision because he had an outstanding career at Creighton, graduated, and signed with the Baltimore Orioles.

He played hard in the Baltimore organization, but didn't get anywhere. He continued, however, to show great character and leadership. In talking to Roland Hemond, the General Manger of the Orioles and long time friend of mine, I found out that Fleita's career was stalling. In light of this information, I recommended that he consider Fleita for a position in player development. After that, Oneri had a very successful career as a field manager in the Orioles' organization. When Jim Hendry became the Director of Scouting with the Chicago Cubs, he hired Fleita as a scout. Eventually, Fleita became Vice President of Player Personnel.

The player development program under Jim Hendry and Oneri Fleita is considered, by professionals in the industry, to be one of the most productive in baseball. Oneri Fleita is a good example of a player that kept a good attitude even when he was on the bench. In addition, he didn't burn the bridges behind him. This attitude opened many doors for him and will continue to serve him well as he climbs the ladder in professional baseball.

Al Powell

Coaching college baseball is like a rollercoaster ride. You have your ups and downs. Every coach needs someone to vent their emotional anxieties to. Many times this person is your wife, and in my case, Rosetta was great. Beyond that there are more people you confide in. Al Powell, one of the greatest people I have ever known, was a very close confidant of mine.

Al was a very successful race car driver from the Miami area. I met him because our sons were both involved in athletics at Columbus High School. To understand my relationship with Al, it is essential that I tell you of his own career.

Al was a great in the sport of racing, where he had few peers. One weekend in the early 1950's, Al was to race in a charity event where the proceeds were to go towards providing iron lungs for the local hospitals. The night before the race he came down with a sickness, but he decided to go through with it the next day nevertheless. After the race, Al was admitted to a Miami Hospital and was eventually hooked up to an iron lung and diagnosed with polio. This incident happened before the vaccine was available.

Al became a quadriplegic. Al never lost his positive outlook on life. After the fact he fathered three more children. His upbeat attitude was evident from the first day I met him, later on in the 60's. He and his wife, Betty Ruth, were very active in the social scene at Columbus.

When I would visit with Al at one of our children's baseball games, he was always very positive. He always wanted to know how my teams at Miami Dade were playing. When we lost, he was consoling and he became a counselor for me, giving me suggestions and a psychological lift. When I would talk to him on the phone or in person, and asked him how he was doing, his answer was always, "Great, things couldn't be better." His positive attitude, in light of his special needs, really put winning or losing a baseball game in its proper perspective. I don't ever remember Al being down in the dumps. Without him as an inspirational leader, handling such mundane events as losing a baseball game would have been all but insurmountable. He had a great feel for the game of baseball, but more importantly, a great understanding of the human psyche.

Herb Holmberg was the man who originally introduced me to Al. He and I spent many hours at Al's house fixing our aging automobiles. Al would actually coach us from his wheelchair, on how to replace brake linings, how to perform engine tune-ups, and other related operations.

Years later, when his wife Betty Ruth could not physically handle getting Al in and out of their car, it was clear they needed a van with a lift. Herb and I asked Al if he would allow us to hold a benefit on his behalf in order get this new van. With tears in his eyes, he thanked us and said we could hold the charity function.

We immediately made plans with the administration at Columbus High School to assist us in the project. We set up an Al Powell account and received permission to use the Columbus cafeteria. We contacted Jerry's Caterers, which supplied food to the many airlines going in and out of Miami. Our first request was for them to provide only the food and we would prepare it. Since the owners of Jerry's knew Al, they decided to prepare a nice dinner for the event themselves, free of charge.

We contacted several hundred people via mail, regarding Al Powell Night. The response was overwhelming! It was a great night for a great cause. We bought Al a beautiful Ford van with a hydraulic lift. We even had money left over for him to upgrade the van or use as he saw fit.

Prior to Al getting the van, he had a very active life writing children's books about automobile racing. Later, the Miami Dade Transportation Department ended up employing him as a consultant. He gave them advice regarding providing bus transportation for people with special needs. During his retirement he and Betty Ruth resided in Miami up until their passing away in 2007. At the time of Al's death he was watching the Daytona races on television. Betty Ruth died eight hours later. The family asked me to do the eulogy for Betty Ruth and Al. It was a great assignment for me personally to be able to honor a great couple and to say thanks on behalf of the people whose lives they touched.

I will never forget Al Powell and the impact he had on my life and coaching career. What a winner and role model!

The Mainieri Factor

At my retirement banquet (Left to Right: Betty Ruth and Al Powell, Herb Holmberg, and me).Photo courtesy of Bob Bailey of the Miami Dade Media Dept.

Manny Lopez

One day I received a letter from a man who was an agent for an umpire. This umpire was Manny Lopez. He enclosed a certificate which indicated Manny's completion of an umpire clinic. It was signed by Joe Linsalatta, the coordinator of umpire development for professional baseball. The agent asked if we would be interested in having him work some of our games. I passed the letter on to one of my assistants Nick "the Greek" Siemaz with a notation to check the umpire out. Maybe he could work an exhibition game of ours in early February, 1975.

The University of Miami and Miami Dade both finished second in their respective World Series in 1974. Ron Frasier, head coach at Miami, and I arranged to play a game on our field. In those days junior colleges could play senior colleges.

On the day of the game, for which we had a nice crowd, I arrived late to the field and a couple people, along with the Greek, were helping a special needs person put on his umpiring gear. The umpire had a severe case of cerebral palsy. I asked Siemaz who the umpire was, and he told me it was Manny Lopez. Manny did the plate during the game.

There were several reporters and TV people in attendance. Apparently they were notified by Manny's agent. At any rate, having a person afflicted with cerebral palsy umpire our game was a worthy news item. In fact, it was on local television and the Miami News did a long article about it. The gist of the article was that "Demie Mainieri, who had always been tough on umpires, had mellowed and gave Manny a chance to umpire a college baseball game." The news story went over the wire services. I ended up receiving a letter from Bobo Brayton, a good friend of mine and head coach at Washington State University, with a copy of the article that appeared in the Pullman, Washington newspaper. His note read "Demie, what some coaches will do to get umpires on their side… Your Friend, Bobo."

Sometime later Manny's agent informed me that there was a new procedure on the market, whereby they used a pacemaker with electrodes to the brain in order to calm down the effects of cerebral palsy. The one drawback was that the procedure and device was quite expensive and Manny could not afford it. He had heard the cerebral palsy telethon was going to be televised from Miami Beach Convention Center by Dennis James and he wondered if I might go to the program with Manny, so he could explain the situation and need for funds. I told him I would be happy to accommodate his request. In fact, Dennis James was my first cousin and I would be happy to talk to him before Manny and I went on the telethon.

As a result of the program, he received financial help in order to get the new procedure.

This is another great story of a person whose life was changed because of his positive attitude and the helping hands of others. Manny Lopez is still a resident of Miami and is doing well.

The Mainieri Factor

"Demie, what some coaches will do to get umpires on their side."
Photo courtesy of Bob Bailey MD Media Dept.

Pete Sarron

This player was a co-captain on my 1964 National Champion team. He was a fierce competitor. One day he ran into a palm tree going after a fly ball at a Miami city park. He broke his jaw in the collision. A week after this accident, he was cleared by the doctor, and Pete played with a wired jaw and a batting helmet with a mask. This didn't surprise me because his dad was the former featherweight champion of the world, and I knew the apple didn't fall far from the tree.

I always taught my own children and former players, to never burn the bridges behind you. Someday, someone may call for a recommendation. It is always better to get a good recommendation than a negative response.

Pete graduated from Florida State with a major in criminal justice. He applied to the FBI and was 104th on the prospect list of future agents, which wasn't very good. He came to my office one day and mentioned his dilemma. I told Pete that a good friend and racquetball partner of mine, Ken Whittaker, was the chief of the Miami FBI office. I said I would talk to Ken for him.

Ken came to my office one day before we were to head to the racquetball courts and I mentioned Pete and his strong desire to be an FBI agent. I outlined all of Pete's positive character traits and his competitive drive. Ken called the FBI office in D.C. and spoke highly of Pete. Based on this phone call, Pete was moved from 104th all the way up to number 4. Shortly thereafter, Pete received notice to report to Quantico, Virginia.

Pete spent two or three years in the Detroit office. After that he became a narcotics agent. This shows how good things happen to good people who do not burn the bridges left behind them.

Nellie Mitchell

This fine player was one of the first recruits I signed out of Miami Norland High School. He wasn't a great player but he loved the game, played hard, and was dependable. As left-handed hitter, he sure wore out the left field line! He tried to use the whole field, hit the ball where it was pitched. He finished his career at the University of Miami.

After graduating from Miami, I assisted him in getting a baseball graduate assistantship under my good friend, Bob Wren, at Ohio University. Previously, I had sent a man named Stan Sanders to Bob for a graduate assistantship, and Stan became a full time assistant there. Eventually he became head coach at the University of Toledo. So Bob and I had a good tradition going.

It was no surprise that Nellie had a great experience at Ohio. He received his masters in management under Dr. Jim Mason and Dr. Owen Wilkinson. After graduation, he returned to Miami Dade and worked in a variety of positions with distinction.

Miami Area Baseball Clinic (Left to Right: Nellie Mitchell, Mickey Mantle, and me). Courtesy of Bob Bailey MD Media Dept.

Dave Lawson

This individual played for me when I coached at Valley High School in Masontown, West Virginia. The previous coach at Valley had only negative comments about Dave's general attitude, off the field activities, and performance in the class room. He said he was a very talented athlete that needed discipline. He was right in all areas.

Once I outlined what I expected of him, Dave's attitude changed. He became a great individual to coach. He went on to play basketball at the University of Tampa, a very good and well respected program at the time.

After receiving his masters from West Virginia University, I hired him as an athletic trainer at Miami Dade. Years later, he became a quadriplegic and passed away while living at a nursing home in Tennessee. He had matured into a fine athlete, but more importantly, a fine person with a strong faith.

Tony Segreto

One day I received a phone call from Bernie Rosen, of the sports department at the NBC affiliate in Miami. He asked me to help get a fellow, Tony Segreto, registered at Miami Dade. He had attended St. Leo College in Dade City, Florida, but wanted to enroll at Miami Dade and work part time at WTVJ. I was able to get Tony in classes at times that worked with his schedule at the station. This was a small favor on my part, but it did get Tony started in the right direction.

Tony's rise, under Bernie's mentoring, was quick through the ranks at the station. He was sports commentator for several years and is now the news anchor at WTVJ. I am happy to have Tony as my friend and to know I had a small hand in his success. This goes to show the importance of networking.

Rich Garcia

We were playing Florida Keys Community College in Key West. Rich Garcia was the home plate umpire and I thought he was calling a very good game. Key West had a reputation for having difficulty getting unbiased umpires because of its isolated location, but Rich, a local resident, was doing a very honest job. In the 9th inning, there was a bang-bang play at home plate and Rich called the Key West base runner out. We won the game by one run. The coach from Florida Keys ripped Rich pretty good, using language that is beyond description here.

After the game, Rich came by the Holiday Inn Lounge where my staff and I were having some post game food and drink. I said to him, "Rich, I really have to commend you for the good job you did tonight. You are honest, have good judgment, and have guts. But you have to one of the dumbest guys around to make that call against Florida Keys, considering you have to live in this town."

I told him I would call Ed Doherty, administrator of Major League Umpire Development, so that I could recommend him as a prospective professional umpire. I talked to Mr. Doherty and he mentioned that Joe Linsalatta, his field director, would call me for the details on Rich. Mr. Linsalatta told me he would contact Rich so that he could place him in the development program.

After working under Joe Linsalatta's tutelage, Rich Garcia umpired for four years in the minors before being called up to the major leagues. He spent over ten years as a big league umpire. He presently is a supervisor of major league umpires. Our paths have crossed several times and he never fails to mention how I got him started in professional umpiring. I might add that Rich used some good common sense and moved from Key West and is now resident of Clearwater, Florida.

Don Baylor

Don Baylor was a rookie player in the Orioles organization. Harry Dalton was the GM of the Baltimore club. Harry and I were good friends, ever since we both worked on the Professional Baseball-College Baseball Relations Committee. In addition, the Orioles also trained at Biscayne College (St. Thomas University), which was close to Miami Dade. In the past, Harry had invited Miami Dade to play exhibitions against his minor league teams.

At any rate, I received a call from Harry one day asking if I would do him a favor. He had a young player by the name of Don Baylor that he placed in a National Guard Unit adjacent to Miami Dade (many young people during the Vietnam War joined the National Guard to delay entering Military service, so long as they were enrolled in college). Harry mentioned that Baylor would only move to Miami during the off season and would attend monthly National Guard meetings if he could also attend college. Harry wanted to know if I could get Don enrolled at Miami Dade immediately. I said I'd try, but the fall semester had already begun three weeks prior! He said if anyone could pull it off, it would be Demie Mainieri. The pressure was on.

I talked to five teachers about allowing Don to register for their courses. Naturally, Don would have to make up the work he had missed. At the end of the semester, the professors told me Don was a very dependable student, made up the missed work, and generally did well.

Don Baylor had a very productive major league career and managed the Rockies and the Cubs. In the media guides of these two clubs, they mentioned he attended Miami Dade. Don and I remain close friends.

Richard Bancells

Besides my duties at Miami Dade, I was an adjunct professor in sports management at St Thomas. In my introductory comments about how one gets started in athletics, I emphasized that one needs to come up with a marketable skill or special talent. Many times, the only way to get the necessary experience in some facet of sports management is to volunteer at some major league front office or college athletic department. After class, Rich Bancells, a student, introduced himself to me and wanted to know more specifics on how he could volunteer and get this needed experience. I mentioned that he could volunteer to work with our athletic trainer at Miami Dade. He jumped on the opportunity and worked very nicely with the trainer, Dave Lawson.

During Richard's second year of volunteering, Dave was having difficulty handling all the duties of the head trainer. Dave had neurological problems, resulting from a previous operation on his cervical spine. In light of this, I was able to create a "full time-part time" situation for Richard. In other words, I could place him on the payroll without benefits, e.g. health care, retirement, and the like.

Tom Giordano, director of player development for the Baltimore Orioles, called me with a request to recommend a young athletic trainer he could employ for his Bluefield, West Virginia club in the Appalachian League.

I recommended Rich very highly because he had really progressed as a trainer. After three or four years in the minors, Rich was promoted to the position of Head Athletic Trainer for the Orioles major league club. He has held this position with distinction for several years. This movement up the ladder of success was result of hard work and capitalizing on the window of opportunity open to him.

Paul Mainieri's Stories

Mike Kazlausky

Mike was on the team during my early years at the Air Force Academy. Mike did not have outstanding natural ability, but he played the game with a great deal of hustle and pride. I don't think I have ever coached a guy that played harder than Mike. I never once saw him get out of the way of a pitch. Once it hit him, he'd throw his bat down and sprint to first base. He'd move so quick that sometimes the umpire and catcher would fall all over themselves trying to reach him because they thought he was charging the mound. Every time Mike hit a home run, he'd be around the bases so fast that he'd touch home plate before the team would be out of the dugout to congratulate him. His effort wasn't restricted only to the nine innings of a game either. After infield and batting practice he'd be so dirty and cut up from diving for balls, it looked like he had just played a whole game. Mike is a shining example of how the game of baseball should be played.

Steve Stanley

Show me a player that does more things for his team on a consistently high level, and I will be the first one to shake that young man's hand. He has many great attributes, but his heart may be the most important. There is a great deal of players with great talent that never come close to making an impact on their team like he did.

Steve got off to an awful start his freshman season. After starting 0-17 he met with me in my office because he was worried he might be benched. I said to him, "Steve, what do you think is the most important thing you can do for this team?"

He replied, "Get hits?"

I said, "No, not at all. The most important thing you can do for this team is catch the ball in centerfield. Now, what do you think is the second most important thing you can do?"

"Get hits?"

"No. The next thing is to get on base. Get on base any way you can. Draw walks, leg some balls out, bunt for hits, anything you can do to get on. What about the next thing?"

"Get some hits?"

"No, Steve, no. The next thing you can do is once you get on base, steal some bases. Use your speed to help us out on the base paths. What next?"

"Hits?"

"Nope. The next thing you need to do is bring that feistiness, that competitive spirit you possess to the team and instill it in everybody else. Ok, what next?"

"I don't know, Coach."

I said, "Get some hits once in a while!"

After that Steve only went on to become 3rd all time for career hits in the NCAA. He was drafted in the 2nd round and continued to make progress in his professional career until his retirement so he could spend more time with his wife and baby.

Brad Lidge

This young man came to Notre Dame from Cherry Creek High School in Denver, Colorado, where he was an outfielder, not stepping on the mound till his senior year. And even then, the amount he pitched was minimal. At the end of his freshman fall, I posted a depth chart in the clubhouse. Brad was ranked 17th among the pitchers. We had only 17 pitchers.

He came to me and said he was better than that. He said he was going to show me he was better than that, too. I said ok, Brad. Let's see it.

And, well, everything after that is history. He became one of the dominant starters in the Big East Conference. He was drafted in the first round by the Astros in his junior year. You know him now as one of the best, if not the very best, relief pitchers in the major leagues.

Brad Lidge- closer for the Astros- Photo courtesy of Houston Astros

Aaron Heilman

You all know Aaron now as a pitcher for the New York Mets. While he was with us at Notre Dame, he notoriously had bad falls. Fall practice is really the only time we get outside to practice before our first game in the spring, so I do a lot of evaluating and determining who can play for us during that time. Every year, Aaron had a terrible fall practice.

After his junior year, Aaron turned down over a million dollars to come back to school for his senior year. Like always, he had a terrible fall. Before he went home for Thanksgiving, I said to him, "Come back out to the field and throw one more bullpen. I have to make sure you still have it."

We did it at night, with all the lights on, out on the field on the main mound. Nobody but him, a catcher, and me on the field. He threw great, of course. I asked him what the deal was during the fall.

"It's like this, Coach," he said. "I need to see a batter in a different uniform for me to get my juices going. All fall, I'm pitching to our own batters and that just doesn't do it for me. Also, I need to be able to pitch inside to be effective. What happens if I hit one of our batters on the hand in the fall? What good would that do?"

After hearing that, I knew he still had it and was ready. He went 15-0 that season. He ended his career at Notre Dame with a 43-7 record and a career 425 strike outs.

On April 15, 2005, Aaron pitched a one-hitter against the Florida Marlins. It was only fitting that the catcher for that game was Mike Piazza, who played for my dad at Miami-Dade.

Matt Nussbaum

Matt started his career at Notre Dame as an unheralded walk-on infielder. At the end of his sophomore fall, I told him that my goal was for him to win a letter by the end of his career. A very modest goal to say the least.

That year, we had a left-handed dominant lineup and by the 6th game of the season, I put Matt in the game just to get a righty in there. Matt took advantage of the opportunity. That game he hit two home runs and played great. He was in the lineup for the rest of his career. He became one of our captains in his last season.

He is a tremendous role model for young, aspiring ball players. He shows that through dedication, hard work, and a positive attitude, one can be successful, taking advantage of the opportunities when you get them.

Chapter 8

The Relationship between Amateur Baseball and Professional Baseball: The Role of the Scout, the Coach and Parents

WHAT FOLLOWS IS AN article I wrote for *Coaching Digest*, which was published by the American Baseball Coaches Association, in February of 1999.

Preface

The writer developed this paper since he has been on both sides of the fence; therefore, he has a rather unique perspective regarding this subject. The writer was a college coach for thirty years and a full-time scout with the Milwaukee Brewers for the last eight years. During his tenure as a college coach, the writer had very few negative experiences with full or part-time scouts. This cooperation resulted in 30 of the writer's former players making it to the major leagues. The most notable players making it to the big leagues were: **Bucky Dent and Mickey Rivers (Yankees); Mike Piazza (Mets); Steve Carlton (Phillies); Randy Bush (Twins); John Cangelosi (Marlins); Warren**

Cromartie (Expos); Kurt Bevacqua (Padres); Odibbe McDowell and Pat Putnam (Rangers); Tim Hutlett (Orioles); Bob Stinson (Mariners); Ray Bare (Tigers); and numerous others. In addition, many other players had a chance to fulfill their dreams of a professional career because of this cooperation. In many cases, the area scout that signed these players to fill roster spots did so as a favor to him because of his cooperation.

Introduction:

There appears to be a growing strained relationship between coaches and professional scouts. It has become rather common to hear such horror stories— e.g. professional scouts calling coaches during the dinner hours, late at night, or during school hours when the coach was teaching class. There have been some cases where scouts berated coaches in front of their teams for not cooperating with the scouts. Some associate scouts, who are also referred to as "bird dogs," work for full-time scouts. These associate scouts receive a small stipend if the prospect they recommend to the area scout remains in professional baseball for 60 days. These gentlemen are providing this service because most of them love the game of baseball. A few of these individuals may, at times, use poor judgment and overstep their responsibilities. Some coaches, on the other hand, are not providing rosters, schedules, and giving pitching assignments to the scouts.

Unfortunately, it is easy for coaches to generalize negatively about scouts not acting professionally. On the other hand, the same is true of scouts generalizing negatively about coaches because one or two do not cooperate. It is to the point that the present environment is not serving well the game of baseball and the players. In most cases, these antagonisms only exacerbate the problem, and in the final analysis, hurt the players who may have the potential to play professional baseball. It is a very sad situation needing correcting.

Basic Assumptions:

The professional scouts have the responsibility to identify potential professional baseball prospects, to determine their eligibility, to determine what round the player should be drafted, and ultimately to sign the player(s).

The coach is, first and foremost, an educator. His responsibility is to develop the player, under his tutelage, to be the best player he can be. He has the responsibility to help players develop skills necessary to handle the exigencies of life and know the importance of an education. In some situations, he must win and have a successful program in order to retain his position. As an educator, he has the right and responsibility to give the players the pros and cons of going into professional baseball, as opposed to going to and staying in college. He has the responsibility of giving players both viewpoints rather than attempting to influence the individual in one direction. This is an awesome responsibility. Coaches should be cognizant of the fact that the player should have the ultimate responsibility for making the final decision, since he must live that decision.

Recommendations to Improve the Scout/Coach Relationship:

Scouts:
1. **Always handle your responsibilities in a professional manner.** Realize that the coach has a job to do just as you have a job to perform.
2. **As a courtesy, ask permission of the coach to come into the dugout and/or onto the field.** Act as though you are a guest of the coach's domain.
3. **Ask permission of the coach to talk to a player.** Be diplomatic in your request. Ask the coach when the best time is and place to talk to the player. Avoid talking to the player on game days unless the coach suggests it. Coaches may interpret that you are acting secretly if you do not channel contacts with players through the coach.

4. **Request schedules, rosters, and lineups at the appropriate time.** You may be able to get pitching rotations, schedules, statistics, and other pertinent information on the Internet. You can also communicate with the coach via e-mail. Ask the coach for his e-mail address and give him yours. Do not make requests for a lineup too early or too late before game time.
5. **Scouts should not telephone the coach early in the morning, late at night, or during the dinner hour.** You must realize that coaches have family responsibilities once they are home. Never call after 9:00 p.m. If you leave a message for the coach to call you back with information, leave your voice mail number; most high school coaches may not telephone by long distance, and college coaches may be on a tight schedule.
6. **If you have a conflict with a coach, try to settle it on a face to face basis and at a time when both you and the coach have calmed down.** Never berate or argue with a coach in front of his team and fans.
7. **Scouts should share information only when a particular player is going to pitch so that telephone calls to the coach are minimal.**
8. **Never call a coach at his school and request that you talk to him when he is in a meeting or teaching a class.** Keep in mind, most high school coaches have teaching responsibilities besides coaching. In fact, most attain tenure on their teaching ability and not necessarily their coaching record.
9. **Refrain from telephoning a player too frequently to request information from him.** This practice tends to be disruptive to many players. Many times they do not understand the relationship with scouts and might tend to press when they play. In some cases, they may very well get an inflated opinion of their ability and worth. As we all know, many times you may not even draft the player that you have often called. This may make it difficult for the club that eventually drafts and tries to sign him.

Coaches:

1. **Be courteous to scouts.** Visit with the scouts to find out if they need any additional information on players. It is important to realize that they have a job to perform as well as you do. For these scouts, this is their livelihood. Their evaluations depend on the number of prospects they can find and ultimately sign to professional contracts. In the present climate, many of the scouts have attended college, or in some cases are college graduates. They are very much in tune with the importance of a college education; however, they are duty bound to present the benefits of a professional baseball career. The coach, as an educator, has the responsibility to inform the player of the importance of an education. Respect the scouts position and you will find that most scouts will respect your role as well. Remember that the greatest concern is the player's welfare. Turn off the scout, and you may very well hurt your players in the long run.
2. **Provide the scouts with a roster that includes full name, weight, and height, and position, date of birth, home address, telephone number, and year in school.** Providing this information will reduce the necessity of scouts having to bother you requesting additional information. You might also want to provide the names of the head coach and/or assistant coach(s) with their work and home telephone numbers and times when it is convenient to call. In order to avoid annoying telephone calls, leave messages on your answering machine relative to when a particular player is going to pitch. If you do not have an answering machine, indicate the phone number of a secretary the scout can call and the secretary can provide the information that you give her. Use this format when making changes to the schedule and there is other pertinent information. Some coaches that have a website may want to enter onto their homepage their pitching rotation, schedules, statistics, and any other information the scout may need. Provide the scout with your email address. The scouts can then request information via this medium. These little chores will substantially reduce the number of annoying telephone calls. Just remember the area scout needs this information to

pass on to the regional and national cross checkers who have to make airline flight plans.
3. **Do not be upset when you lose a player to the professional ranks.** If the entire matter was handled professionally, the scout will invariably recommend your school/college to two or three prospects for every one he signs.
4. **If you have a conflict with a full or part time scout, talk with him on a face-to-face basis at a time when you and the scout have calmed down.** Try to resolve conflicts with the associate scouts in the same manner. If you are not successful, do not hesitate to talk to his immediate supervisor, which is usually the area scout.

Summary Statement:

Life for all concerned can be so much more palatable if the scouts and coaches cooperate. Remember that by and large, all of us are involved in baseball because we love the game. If we truly love baseball and want to help young people, we will do everything in our power to make a working environment pleasant and rewarding for all.

Chapter 9

I Did It My Way

On numerous occasions during my career, I heard the song, "My Way", written by Paul Anka. There are several renditions of "My Way", but my favorite ones were sung by Roy Hamilton, a high school classmate of mine, and Frank Sinatra, a fellow New Jerseyite . These really had the greatest impact on me. As I came down the home stretch of my career, I became even more convinced that the lyrics of this aforementioned song had some relatedness to many of the experiences I had in my life and career. The difficult decisions I had to make, with all the implications and ramifications, appeared to have some similarity to the lyrics in "My Way". In light of this, I would like to quote some of the more appropriate lyrics of this great song by Paul Anka.

> I've lived a life that's full.
> I've traveled each and every highway;
> But more, much more than this,
> I did it my way.
> I planned each charted course;
> Each careful step along the byway,
> But more, much more than this,

> **I did it my way.**
> **To say the things he truly feels;**
> **And not the words of one that knells.**
> **The record shows I took the blows**
> **And did it my way!**

In today's society, more people in leadership roles make decisions based on what is politically correct. Some politicians make decisions based on what the polls dictate rather than on what is good for our country. You look at some of our greatest leaders and you can see it quite easily. That wasn't their style.

Harry S Truman said that "The buck stops here." He was talking about not passing the responsibility onto others when you need to make a tough decision. One wonders how many more of our young servicemen would have lost their lives had he not possessed the courage to order dropping the atomic bomb. No one likes wars especially when so many human beings are in harms way, many young lives are lost, and sorrow is brought to so many. The planning and decisions for the Normandy invasion were made by a great leader, General Dwight D. Eisenhower. This decision was made in order to bring about the end of the war in the swiftest fashion. Presidents like Ronald Reagan, Franklin Roosevelt, made many difficult decisions while under tremendous pressure. Their decisions weren't easy.

Although not as much was at stake and the times weren't as grave, Vince Lombardi was also a great leader of men who made the tough decisions he needed to make. Many of these decisions were not readily accepted by team members, but in later years, his former players had only praise for his leadership.

Parents, every day, make tough decisions when raising their children. I refer to these kinds of decisions as "tough love."

These examples, in no way, are meant to characterize the writers of the book you now hold in your hands as peers of these other leaders. I gave you these examples to show you some figures who exemplify the qualities necessary to be a strong leader.

At my retirement banquet in 1991, a video presentation was shown, highlighting my life and career at Miami Dade. This video was developed by the Miami Dade media department with Dr. Mary Mahan and Dr. John Takovich providing the material and acting as advisors. Having worked with me for years, they felt that "My Way" was appropriate background music for the video.

As I sat on the dais, listening to Frank sing, I couldn't help but think of my early life and how my dear mother had a strong influence on my future. My mother always preached that it was important to be a truthful, upright person. She always told me to tell people your true feelings, rather than put on a façade and then talk about them behind their back. At that moment, "My Way" brought back the memories of many decisions I had to make relating to my administrative and coaching positions at Miami Dade. Many times, I knew beforehand that the decisions I made would have a profound impact on people's lives. The same was true when I had to be straight forward with my players. I know that doing it "my way" was not immediately understood or appreciated, but over the years many former players have expressed thanks for my being up front and honest with them.

In May of 2005, my last great baseball team, the 1974 club, had a reunion in Sarasota, Florida. It was a very emotional, yet happy occasion when the players, thirty one years later, wanted to say thanks for doing it my way. They all said, to a man, that they needed that kind of approach since it was during a very formative and impressionable time of their lives.

I did it my way. Whether or not it is the right way can only be determined by the lives you touch. I always asked my players, the coaches, and myself to look at the guy in the mirror. *You've passed the most dangerous and difficult test, if the man in glass is your friend.*

I didn't post too many motivational slogans on my bulletin boards, but the following poem, given to me by my brother Sonny when I was a youngster, did appear.

The Guy in the Mirror

**When you get what you want in the struggle of life and the world makes you King for a day,
Go to the mirror and look at yourself, and see what that guy has to say.
For it's not your father or mother or wife whose judgment you must pass,**

The fellow, whose verdict counts most in this life, is the one staring back from the glass.
Some people may think you're a straight shooting chum, and call you a wonderful guy,
But the man in the glass says you're only a bum, if you can't look him straight in the eye.
He is the fellow to please, never mind all the rest, for he's with you clear up to the end,
And you've passed the most dangerous and difficult test, if the man in the glass is your friend.
You may fool the world down the pathway of years, and get patted on the back as you pass,
But your final reward will be heartache and tears, if you've cheated the man in the glass.
-Author Unknown.

Do it your way, because your team and your organization should reflect your personality. Visit the guy in the mirror and you will know if your way was the right way.

What your mind believes, the body achieves.

The Final Word

After reading the final draft of this manuscript and its ramifications, I thought it appropriate that I recapitulate the toast I gave at the Demie Mainieri Testimonial on February 22, 1991 at the Radisson Mart Plaza Hotel. Here is the entire toast.

Ladies and Gentleman, when Jay Rokeach called me earlier this week in Colorado to ask me if I would be willing to give the final toast tonight, I thought to myself that there is no greater honor for a son than to be given the opportunity to toast the greatest man he has ever known on the night his father is being honored by his friends, colleagues, and family. This opportunity is the highlight of my life.

And so, Dad, I speak for your children and all your former players as I offer this toast. (Raise your glass).

To the man who taught us toughness yet emphasized love of his fellow man.

To the man who taught us how to be competitive, yet compassionate.

To the man who taught us how to deal with failure, yet never get use to losing

To the man who taught us to put God and family above everything else in life.

To the man who taught us to only have to answer to one person, the man in the mirror.

To the greatest educator God put on earth to teach young people.

The late great football Vince Lombardi once said, "The quality of a man's Life is in direct proportion to the intensity of his commitment".

Well Dad, there's never been anyone more committed to his profession of teaching young people how to be successful in life than you!

And there's never been anyone more committed to his colleagues, his friends, his sisters and brothers, his children, or his wife than you.

Your life sets the standard for quality!

And so, for all you are and for all you've been to everyone whose lives have been blessed by your impact on them, I offer this toast for my father,

Demie John Mainieri.

An Assortment of other photographs-Photos courtesy of Bob Bailey of the Miami Dade Media Dept.

Above left: Me at retirement banquet.

Above right: Me, Larry Bowa, Pete Rose, Greg Lazinski, and Tony Simone at Mainieri Field.

Major League players at Miami Dade's Kids' Baseball Clinic. (Above, L to R: Bucky Dent, Bill Lee, Rick Cerone, Gary Carter, Warren Cromartie, Me, Davey Lopes, Steve Nicosia. Bottom, L to R: Me, Rick Cerone, Bucky Dent, Roy Phillips, Andre Dawson, Tony Perez, Dusty Baker, Kurt Bevacqua, Ed Lynch, Tommy Lasorda).

The Mainieri Factor

Me with Pete Rose and me with Frank Robinson. They came to campus to appear in a Sears's film about the teaching of hitting.

My son Paul honored me by speaking at my retirement banquet. Here he is next to the picture of him as Batboy.

My three sons- (from Left to Right, Jim, John, and Paul, former Miami Dade Batboys).

I threw out the first pitch at Notre Dame-Michigan game in 2004. My grandson Nick caught it-Photo courtesy of Notre Dame Media Department /Athletics

The Mainieri Factor

Demie Mainieri gets the victory ride celebrating the win that made the Falcon head coach the first junior college baseball coach in the nation to win 1,000 games in a career.

Sophomore pitcher Nick McClellen (R) was the winning pitcher in the 6-0 blanking of the United States Naval Academy.

South Florida media surround Demie Mainieri after career win #1000.

University of Miami head baseball coach Ron Fraser (L) and M-DCC North head man Demie Mainieri have won over 2000 games in their storied careers.

U.S. Navy head coach Joe Duff congratulates M-DCC North baseball coach Demie Mainieri following 6-0 victory.

Demie Mainieri and long time assistant coach Tony Simone with plaque honoring Mainieri on his career win #1000.

Epilogue

Since the time this manuscript was completed, some changes have occurred.

Paul, after twelve years at Notre Dame, accepted in July, 2006, the position of Head Baseball Coach at LSU. This was a difficult decision for Paul, since he had a very successful career at Notre Dame. Leaving all of his friends in the Notre Dame and South Bend communities was the hardest. The move was made even more trying since his daughter Sami is a Notre Dame cheerleader. Nick has been employed as an Administrative Assistant to Notre Dame Head Football Coach, Charlie Weis. Alexandra is a senior at Ball State University.

Paul and his coaching staff are faced with a tremendous challenge to elevate the LSU baseball program to the elite status it experienced under Stanley "Skip" Bertman

Randy Bush, who played on two World Series Championship Minnesota Twins teams, was promoted to Assistant General Manager of the Chicago Cubs in 2005.

About the Authors

Demie Mainieri

Dr. Manieri, seventy-eight years old, was Director of Athletics and Head Baseball Coach at Miami Dade North for thirty years.

Demie Mainieri was the first junior college baseball coach to win 1000 games. Thirty of his former players made it to the major leagues. Steve Carlton has been inducted into the Hall of Fame in Cooperstown, New York. Over one hundred were drafted or signed by professional teams. One hundred and fifty received senior college scholarships. Many of his former players are now doctors, lawyers, college professors, teachers, coaches, FBI and other law enforcement agents and many more exciting professions.

His Miami Dade baseball team won the 1964 NJCAA National Championship, three second place finishes and one third in the NJCAA World Series in Grand Junction, Colorado.

He was head coach for the USA Junior National team that won the 1980 World Championship in Venezuela. In 1978 he was on the staff that placed second at the World Games in Italy (forerunner of the Olympic Games).

Coach Mainieri was inducted into six Hall of Fames besides being selected to the NJCAA All Century team.

He was an Adjunct Professor (Sports Administration) at St. Thomas University in Miami, Florida and The USA Sports Academy in Daphne, Alabama. Since his retirement in 2001 to the present, he has worked for the Milwaukee Brewers, Florida Marlins, and the Chicago Cubs as a Special Assignment Scout. He and his wife reside in Fort Lauderdale, Florida.

Paul Mainieri

Paul Mainieri has had a varied and successful career as a college head baseball coach. After two years in the Chicago White Sox organization, he was an assistant football and baseball coach at his alma mater Columbus High School. He then worked his way up the ladder with head coaching stints of six years at St, Thomas University in Miami, Florida and the Air Force Academy. In addition, he had twelve very successful years as the Head Baseball Coach at the University of Notre Dame. In the summer of 2007, he was selected the new Head Baseball Coach at LSU. With 983 college wins already he should hit the 1000 win plateau during the LSU 2008 season. He is very committed to returning the LSU baseball program to the elite status they had under Skip Bertman. Fifty of Mainieri's Notre Dame players were drafted or signed as free agents. Eighteen of his players were drafted in the first twenty rounds of the draft. His Irish players also combined for fourteen All America and ten Academic All America seasons. While at Notre Dame, he had a 100% graduation rate of those players that completed their collegiate eligibility.

Under coach Mainieri's leadership, Notre Dame was one of just four colleges from 1998-2001 that produced two pitchers, Brad Lidge (!998, Houston Astros) and Aaron Heilman (2002, NY Mets) who were drafted in the first round. They both were able to make it to the Major Leagues. Mainieri and his staff have molded players into top prospects, as Lidge was just a forty-second pick out of high school while Heilman was a fifty-four round pick.

Paul Mainieri and wife Karen have four children and reside in Baton Rouge, Louisiana.

Printed in the United States
208085BV00002B/186/A